797,885 Books
are available to read at

www.ForgottenBooks.com

Forgotten Books' App
Available for mobile, tablet & eReader

ISBN 978-1-330-78178-4
PIBN 10104664

This book is a reproduction of an important historical work. Forgotten Books uses state-of-the-art technology to digitally reconstruct the work, preserving the original format whilst repairing imperfections present in the aged copy. In rare cases, an imperfection in the original, such as a blemish or missing page, may be replicated in our edition. We do, however, repair the vast majority of imperfections successfully; any imperfections that remain are intentionally left to preserve the state of such historical works.

Forgotten Books is a registered trademark of FB &c Ltd.
Copyright © 2015 FB &c Ltd.
FB &c Ltd, Dalton House, 60 Windsor Avenue, London, SW19 2RR.
Company number 08720141. Registered in England and Wales.

For support please visit www.forgottenbooks.com

1 MONTH OF FREE READING

at
www.ForgottenBooks.com

By purchasing this book you are eligible for one month membership to ForgottenBooks.com, giving you unlimited access to our entire collection of over 700,000 titles via our web site and mobile apps.

To claim your free month visit:
www.forgottenbooks.com/free104664

* Offer is valid for 45 days from date of purchase. Terms and conditions apply.

English
Français
Deutsche
Italiano
Español
Português

www.forgottenbooks.com

Mythology Photography **Fiction**
Fishing Christianity **Art** Cooking
Essays Buddhism Freemasonry
Medicine **Biology** Music **Ancient Egypt** Evolution Carpentry Physics
Dance Geology **Mathematics** Fitness
Shakespeare **Folklore** Yoga Marketing
Confidence Immortality Biographies
Poetry **Psychology** Witchcraft
Electronics Chemistry History **Law**
Accounting **Philosophy** Anthropology
Alchemy Drama Quantum Mechanics
Atheism Sexual Health **Ancient History**
Entrepreneurship Languages Sport
Paleontology Needlework Islam
Metaphysics Investment Archaeology
Parenting Statistics Criminology
Motivational

THE LAW OF ARREST

IN

CIVIL AND CRIMINAL ACTIONS

BY

HARVEY CORTLANDT VOORHEES

OF THE BOSTON BAR

BOSTON
THE BOSTON BOOK COMPANY
1904

Entered according to Act of Congress, in the year 1904,
BY HARVEY CORTLANDT VOORHEES,
In the Office of the Librarian of Congress, at Washington.

THE UNIVERSITY PRESS, CAMBRIDGE, U. S. A.

PREFACE

In the preparation of this treatise the writer has endeavored to produce a work so exhaustive that the profession might feel justified in pronouncing it a standard authority on the subject with which it deals. At the same time it has been the effort to produce a work of such simple style that it would be intelligible to those not versed in legal lore, and that the many officers of the law who are called upon to invade the sacred right of personal liberty might do so with a full understanding of the rights of the accused, as well as their own rights.

On the points of law where the cases are not in harmony, and cannot be reconciled, as, for example, whether, at common law, a seal was essential to the validity of a warrant, a careful examination of the decisions has been made, and what has appeared to be the better reasoning and weight of authority has been presented.

The citations, covering the best decisions of both English and American courts, have been selected with view of making the work exceedingly useful as a general treatise on this important subject in the different States.

HARVEY CORTLANDT VOORHEES.

Boston, Mass., *May* 1, 1904.

31-YEAR-OLD FORMULA OF THE UNIVERSITY OF MISSOURI-ROLLA

CONTENTS

                                                            PAGE

TABLE OF CASES ix

CHAPTER I.

THE RIGHT OF PERSONAL LIBERTY 1

    Definition. — Magna Charta. — Petition of Right. — Act of 1664. — Habeas Corpus Act. — English Bill of Rights. — Excessive Bail Prohibited. — American Bill of Rights. — Due Process of Law. — The Limit of Governmental Control.

CHAPTER II.

THE ISSUANCE AND SERVICE OF LEGAL PROCESS . 8

    Definition. — Jurisdiction. — Procured by Stratagem and Fraud. — Procured by Illegal Arrest. — Foreign Vessels. — Ceded Territory. — Search Warrant. — Illegal Seizure does not affect Admissibility of Evidence procured thereby. — Bench Warrant. — Warrant of Arrest. — What Officer Must Know. — Necessity of Return. — Life of Warrant. — Requisites of a Valid Warrant. — When Valid without Seal.

CHAPTER III.

WHO MAY ISSUE A WARRANT 32

    Mandamus. — Complaint. — Necessary Evidence. — Constitutional Provision. — To Whom Directed. — Private Person. — Officer. — Delegating Authority to Serve. — Arrest for Contempt.

CHAPTER IV.

WHAT CONSTITUTES AN ARREST 39

    Definition. — Authority. — Necessary Acts. — Control. — Words of Arrest. — Touching. — Time of Arrest. — Place of Arrest. — Notice of Authority. — Resisting Arrest. — Officer's Duty After Arrest. — Escape. — Liability of Officer.

CHAPTER V.

ARREST WITH WARRANT 56

    Party Named. — Officer's Protection. — Valid Warrant. — Void Warrant. — Taking Life. — Interference. — Liability of Officer's Assistants. — Taking Prisoner before a Magistrate. — Officer's Right to Release Prisoner. — Officer's Right to Detain Prisoner. — Impossibility as a Defence. — Place of Confinement. — Exercise of Officer's Judgment. — Civil Arrest. — Debtors. — Fraud. — Affidavit.

CHAPTER VI.

ARREST WITHOUT A WARRANT 68

    Private Person. — Felony. — Resisting Private Person. — Hue and Cry. — What is a Felony. — Misdemeanor. — What is Breach of the Peace. — Use of Force. — Officer. — Violation of City Ordinance. — Presence. — Outside of Jurisdiction. — Entering Doors. — Entering House to Arrest for Peaceable Drunkenness. — Deserters from Army. — Arrest to Prevent Crime.

CHAPTER VII.

BREAKING DOORS TO MAKE AN ARREST 89

    Man's Habitation is Sacred. — Notification, Demand and Refusal. — Civil Process. — Criminal Process. — Private Person's Right to Break. — Who is Protected. — Breaking to Prevent Escape. — Inner Doors. — When Usual Inner Door is Legal Outer Door. — What is a Dwelling House. — Use of Portion as Dwelling. — Combined Residence

CONTENTS. vii

PAGE

and Place of Business. — Effect of Absence. — What is a Breaking. — Doors. — Windows. — Other Openings. — Enlarging Opening. — Entrance by Deception. — Effect of Illegal Breaking on Arrest.

CHAPTER VIII.

FORCE IN THE ACT OF ARREST 104

Killing. — When Justifiable. — Felony. — Misdemeanor. — Resisting Arrest. — Fleeing from Arrest. — Excessive Force. — Right of Officer to Use Club. — Right to Demand Officer's Number. — Use of Handcuffs. — Abuse of Handcuffs.

CHAPTER IX.

DISPOSING OF THE PRISONER 114

Confinement. — Termination of Officer's Control. — Taking through Street Scantily Attired. — Searching the Prisoner. — Removal of Clothing. — What may be Taken from Prisoner. — Physical Examination.

CHAPTER X.

ARREST IN EXTRADITION PROCEEDINGS 120

Extradition and Rendition Distinguished. — Definition. — Authority. — Discharge and Re-arrest. — Examination. — Scope of Habeas Corpus Writ. — Evidence. — Procedure. — Matters Inquired Into. — Comity. — Treaty. — Jurisdiction Procured by Stratagem. — Other Jurisdictional Questions. — Interstate Rendition is Obligatory. — Preliminary Proceedings. — Lies for Crime only. — Who is a Fugitive from Justice.

CHAPTER XI.

EVIDENCE NECESSARY TO ESTABLISH THE OFFENCE 132

Proof Must be Beyond Reasonable Doubt. — Burden of Proof. — Burden of Giving Evidence. — Burden of Proof

Never Shifts. — Presumption of Innocence. — Burden to Show Excessive Force. — Burden to Show Offence in Officer's Presence. — Burden to Show Authority to Arrest. — Burden to Show License. — Insanity. — Character. — Conduct as Evidence of Guilt. — Possession of Stolen Goods as Evidence. — Intoxication. — Confessions. — Criminal Capacity. — Dying Declarations. — Best Evidence Rule. — Ignorance of the Law May Excuse.

CHAPTER XII.

EXEMPTION FROM ARREST 150

Sovereigns. — Diplomatic Agents. — Commercial Agents. — Government Employees. — Other Exemptions. — When Privilege may be Waived. — Writ of Protection. — Persons Under Guardianship. — Statutory Exemptions.

CHAPTER XIII.

FALSE IMPRISONMENT 160

What Constitutes. — Restraint. — Consent. — Restraint Must be Total. — May be by Words. — Serving Lawful Process Improperly may Constitute. — Party Must be Conscious of Restraint.

CHAPTER XIV.

TRESPASS 167

Definition. — Who is Trespasser. — Trespass *vi et armis*. — Accidental Acts. — Criminal Actions for. — Criminal Intent. — In Arrest for Intoxication. — Private Persons Assisting Officer. — When Liable. — Refusing to Assist. — Trespass *ab initio*.

INDEX 175

TABLE OF CASES

[References are to pages.]

Abbott v. Booth	28	Barnard v. Bartlett	90, 93
Ackerson v. People	139	Barnes v. Peters	96
Adams v. New York	16	Barrett v. Copeland	24
Aga Kurhboolie Mahomed v. Reg.	94	Bass v. State	99
		Basye v. State	138
Agnew v. Jobson	118	Batchelder v. Currier	21
Ahern v. Collins	41	Bates v. Com.	50
Alderich v. Humphrey	41	Beaverts v. State	109, 110
Allen v. Crofutt	173	Beers v. Beers	4
v. Gray	7, 19	Bell v. State	5, 139
v. Martin	93	Bellows v. Shannon	47, 48, 49
v. State	5	Belote v. State	140
v. U. S.	135	Benjamin v. Hathaway	23
Allison v. Rheams	22	Bessey v. Olliott	168
Almy v. Wolcott	66	Beville v. State	79
Amadon v. Mann	66	Bigelow v. Stearns	167
Anderson v. Roundtree	154	Bingham v. State	33
Andrews v. People	143	Bird v. Jones	161
Aneals v. People	138	Birr v. People	136
Angelo v. People	145	Blackwell v. State	118
Appleton v. Hopkins	64	Blake's Case	156
Archibald v. State	146	Blatcher v. Kemp	15
Arneson v. Thorstad	60, 61	Blatt v. McBarron	169
Arnold v. Steeves	47, 50	Blewitt v. Phillips	167
Ashley v. Dundas	59	Blight v. Fisher	155
Ashley's Case	68	Block, In re	130
Attaway v. State	133	Blue v. Com.	23
		Bond v. State	5
Bacon v. U. S.	17	Bonner, In re	27
Baldwin v. Murphy	40	Bookhout v. State	28
Ballard v State	85	Borrego v. Ter.	134
Bane v. Methuen	35	Boutte v. Emmer	79
Bank of Columbia v. Okely	4	Bowling v Com.	37, 109
Barclay v. U. S.	71	Boylston v. Kerr	81
Barker, Ex parte	9	Brewster v. People	160

TABLE OF CASES

[References are to pages.]

Bright v. Patton	78	Chase v. Fish	151, 154, 157
Brock v. Stimson	23, 59, 63, 115, 165, 169	Chastaug v. State	17
Brockway v. Crawford	69	Clark v. Brown	138
Brooks v. Com.	68, 78, 91, 106, 139	v. Cleveland	54
v. State	80	v. Woods	19
Brown v. Beatty	169	Clarke v. May	11, 56
Ex parte	9	Clay v. State	13
v. Getchell	154, 156	v. United States	86
v. Howard	19	Clement v. Dudley	66
In re	127	. v. State	106
v. Kendall	167	Clifford, Ex parte	53
v. Levee Com'rs	4	Cline v. State	141
v. State	5	Clinton v. Nelson	62
v. Weaver	85, 107	Cochran v. Toher	112, 113, 114, 115
Brown's Case	129	Codd v. Cabe	29
Browning v. Abrams	126	Cody v. Abrams	164
Brushaber v. Stegemann	41	Cohen v. Huskisson	74
Bryan v. Bates	76	Cole v. Hindson	27
Bryant v. State	145	v. State	146
Burch v. Franklin	69	Colee v. State	141
Burke v. Bell	60, 114, 115	Collins v. Lean	13, 14
Burley v. Griffith	31	Comer v. Knowles	160, 162
Burns v. Erben	78	Com. v. Acton	17
v. State	106	v. Barhight	35
Burton v. State	143	v. Bishop	146
Butler v. Washburn	53	v. Black	30, 37
Butolph v. Blust	79, 83	v. Borden	35
B. & W. R. Co. v Dana	70	v. Brigham	139
		v. Burroughs	142
CABELL v. Arnold	29	v. Carey	51, 70
Caffrey v. Drugan	63	v. Carroll	70
Cahill v. People	89	v. Casey	145
Cameron v. Lightfoot	22	v. Cheney	77, 170
Campbell v. Sherman	21	v. Choate	134
Canceini v. People	5	v. Conlin	10, 82, 103
Cannon, In re	127, 129	v. Cooley	47, 49, 50
Cantrill v. People	52	v. Coughlin	170
Carlton v. People	134	v. County Prison	90
Carr v. State	69, 78, 126	v. Crotty	25, 26, 28, 57, 58
Carraby v. Davis	65	v. Cullen	142
Carter v. State	100	v. Culver	142
Cary v. State	59	v. Dana	16
Caudle v. Seymour	28	v. Doane	148
Chaffee v. Jones	157	v. Dorsey	141
Chandler v. Rutherford	77	v. Drew	57

TABLE OF CASES   xi

[References are to pages]

Com. v. Farrell	53	Com. v. Smith	17
v. Field	37	v. Stebbins	148, 149
v. Foley	74	v. Stephenson	100
v. Foster	15, 28, 36	v. Strupney	101
v. Greer	107	v. Thurlow	136
v. Hagenlock	141	v. Tibbetts	17
v. Haney	146	v. Tobin	23, 78, 81, 172, 173
v. Harris	137		
v. Hastings	165	v. Tracey	52
v. Hawes	125	v. Wait	9
v. Hewes	47, 49	v. Walker	139
v. Holstine	136	v. Ward	28
v. Howe	141	v. Weathers	46, 111
v. Irwin	90	v Wilcox	28
v. Johnston	128	v. Wilson	138
v. Kenney	139	v. Wright	126
v. Knapp	143, 144	Commercial Exch. Bank v. McLeod	117
v. Kosloff	151		
v. Leonard	138	Compton v. Wilder	126
v. Linn	76	Conley v. Com.	141
v. Lucy	14	Connor v. Com.	34
v. Lynn	34	Conoly v. State	43
v. McDermott	139	Conraddy v. People	78, 85, 107
v. McMahon	139	Copeland v. Islay	31
v. McNall	71	Cortez v. State	50
v. Mead	145	Coupal v. Ward	164
v. Mika	146	Courtoy v. Dozier	41
v. Miller	55	Coxson v. Doland	153
v. Montgomery	140	Coyles v. Hurtin	45, 170
v. Moran	28	Crepps v. Durden	21
v. Morihan	52, 115	Croom v. State	69
v. Murray	22	Crosby v. People	140, 141
v. Nickerson	160	Cryer v. State	69, 78
v. O'Brien	137	Curtis v. Hubbard	98, 100
v. O'Connor	76		
v. Phillips	14, 34	DANOVAN v. Jones	77
v. Preece	143	Darling v. Kelly	58
v. Randall	140	Daughdrill v. State	146
v. Redshaw	72	Davidson v. New Orleans	4
v. Reynolds	89, 90, 91, 93	Davis v. Burgess	73
v. Ridgway	84	v. Pac. Tele. Co.	80
v. Roark	19, 23	v. State	95, 96
v. Roberts	146	v. U. S.	69, 77, 136
v. Ruggles	83	Day v. Day	73
v. Sheriff	54, 111	Dehm v. Hinman	23, 36, 112, 116, 171
v. Silvers	72		

TABLE OF CASES

[References are to pages.]

Dennis v. People	100	Farnam v. Feeley	69
Devine, Ex parte	123	Fatheree, Ex parte	145
Devries v. Summit	65	Ferez, In re	121, 122, 124
Dickinson v. Farwell	156	Ferguson v. State	99
Diers v. Mallow	78	Ferrier, Petition of	6
Dietrichs v. Schaw	36, 171	Fetter, In re	128
Dilger v. Com.	80, 106, 107, 109	Field v. Ireland	41
Dillon v. O'Brien	117, 118	Filer v. Smith	77, 78
Dodds v. Board	68	Findlay v. Pruitt	106
Doering v. State	78	Firestone v. Rice	112, 113, 116, 170, 171
Donahoe v. Shed	22, 28		
Doo Woon, In re	9	Fisher v. McGirr	7, 11
Dougherty v. State	170	v. Shattuck	27
Doughty v. State	36	Flagg v. People	143
Douglass v. Barber	78	Fleetwood v. Com.	79
Dow's Case	9	Floyd v. State	54
Doyle v. Russell	55	Ford v. Breen	81
Drennan v. People	18	v. State	139
Duffy v. People	144	Forrester v. Clarke	71
Dunton v. Halstead	158	Forster's Case	107
Dupont v. Pichon	150	Foss, Ex parte	125
Durant, In re	9	v. Hildreth	158
Dwiggins v. Cook	24	Foster v. Neilson	125
Dye v. Com.	148	Frank v. State	100
Dyer v. State	73	Franklin v. State	139
		Frazier v. Turner	19
EAMES v. Johnson	19	French v. Bancroft	43
Earl v. Camp	19	Frost v. Thomas	50
Edginton v. U. S.	138	Fulton v. Staats	77, 106
Edwards v. Elliott	6		
Eilenbecker v. Plymouth Co.	6	GABLICK v. People	140
Ela v. Shepard	19	Galvin v. State	72
Elam v. Lewis	151	Gardner v. Hosmer	24
Elder v. Morrison	171	v. Jessop	152
Emerick v. Harris	4	Garner v. State	137
Emery v. Hapgood	7, 11, 19, 20	Garver v. Ter.	53
v. Chesley	44	Gasset v. Howard	22
Englehardt v. State	141	Gates v. People	144
English v. Caballero	150	Geary v. Stephenson	69
Entick v. Carrington	7, 11	Genner v. Sparks	43, 94
Evans v. State	137, 146	George v. Fellows	159
		v. Radford	40
		Gibson v State	138
FAIRCHILD v. Case	53	Giroux v. State	112
Faire v. State	116	Glazier v. Stafford	152
Farley v. State	132, 135	Godfrey v. State	145

TABLE OF CASES xiii

[References are to pages.]

Gold v. Bissell	19, 41	Head v. Martin	85, 106, 107, 108
Golden v. State	106, 109	Heckman v. Swartz	22
Goldsmith v. Baynard	152	Hedges v. Chapman	77
Gollobitsch v. Rainbow	8	Hedrick v. State	99
Goon Bow v. People	139	Heed v. State	140
Gore v. People	133	Heinrich, In re	122
Grainger v. Hill	42	Heldt v. State	143
Grant v. Shaw	24	Hempstead Co. v. Graves	32
Gravely v. State	133	Henderson v. Com.	74
Gray v. Com.	132	Hensley v. Rose	23
Green v. Kennedy	59	Herring v. Boyle	165, 166
v. Kindy	24	v. State	162
Greenough, In re	128	Hershey v. O'Neill	43
Griffin v. State	139	Heyward, In re	128
Griswold v. Sedgwick	26	Hibbs, Ex parte	125
Groome v. Forrester	7	Hibler v. State	130
Grosvenor v. Inhab. etc.	88	Hill v. People	5, 6
Grumon v. Raymond	14, 28, 58	v. Taylor	43
Guidrat v. People	17	Hines v. Chambers	19
Gurney v. Tufts	7	Hirschmann v. People	138
		Hiss v. Bartlett	154
HABERSHAM v. State	59, 69	Hitchcock v. Baker	54
Hackett v. King	164	v. Holmes	102
Hadley v. Perks	78	Hobart v. Hagget	167
Haggerty v. Wilber	94	Hobbs v. Getchell	157
Hall v. State	138	Hogan v. Stophlet	39
Hallinger v. Davis	5	Hoge v. People	140
Halstead v. Brice	28	Hoke v. Henderson	4
Hamilton v. Calder	77	Holcomb v. Cornish	38, 76
Handcock v. Baker	82, 87, 116	Holland v. State	55, 133
Handley v. State	107	Holley v. Mix	68, 69, 77
Hann v. Lloyd	19	Hollon v. Hopkins	55
Harden v. State	133	Holmes v. Jennison	125
Hardtke v. State	138	Hooker v. Smith	171
Hardy v. Murphy	75	Hopt v. Utah	140, 141, 142
Harft v. McDonald	75	Horton v. Moggridge	152
Harlan, Ex parte	152	Housh v. People	52, 54, 56
Harris v. Hardemann	9	Hubbard v. Garner	117
v. McReynolds	26	v. Mace	94
v. People	5	v. State	75
Harrison v. State	98, 100	Hudson's Case	65
Haskins v. Young	30	Hurn, Ex parte	117
Hathaway v. Johnson	65	Hurtado v. California	4
Hawkins v. Lutton	80	Hussey v. Danforth	67
Hayden v. Songer	36	Hutchinson v. Sangster	59, 60
Hayes v. Mitchell	79		

TABLE OF CASES

[References are to pages.]

MASON v. Cope	110
Ingle v. Bell	71
Inglis v. Sailors Snug Harbor	150
JACKSON v. State	107
v. Wood	4
James v. State	106
Jamison v. Gaernett	79
Jenkins v. State	141
Jennings v. Fundeburg	168
Johnson v. State	28
v. Stewart	26
v. Tompkins	162
Johnston v. Com.	102
Jones v. Jones	41, 42
v. Perry	4
v. Robbins	4
v. State	31, 52, 133
Jourdan v. Donahue	129
Journey v. Sharpe	41
Joyce v. Parkhurst	82
Judson v. Reardon	59, 79
KAINE, In re	125
Keating v. People	140
Keith v. Tuttle	46
Kelsey v. Parmalee	15
Kendall v. U. S.	9
Kennedy v. Dunclee	22
v. State	68
Kent v. Miles	61
Ker v. Illinois	10, 126, 127
v. People	9
Kerbey v. Denbey	103
Kernan v. State	43
Kimball, In re	152
Kindred v. Stitt	47, 69, 114
King v. Berchet	4
v. Ward	172
Kirbie v. State	30, 37, 77
Kirk v. Garrett	77
Kleinschmidt v. Dunphy	5
Knot v. Gay	71
Kurtz v. Moffitt	86
LAGRAVE'S Case	9
Lake's Case	24
Lancaster v. State	141
Lander v. Miles	106
Lannock v. Brown	90
Lascelles v. Georgia	126
v. State	126
League v. State	5
Ledbetter v. State	31, 46
Lee v. State	116, 132
Leggat v. Tollervey	17
Leigh v. Cole	112, 113, 118
v. Webb	13
Leighton, Ex parte	156
Levi, Ex parte	46, 155
Levy v. Edwards	110
Lewis v. City of Raleigh	62
v. State	47, 78
Liggitt v. People	136
Linehan v. State	139
Lockwood v. Coysgarne	150
Loegrove v. State	136
Long v. State	68, 85
Lopez & Sattler's Case	9
Lott v. Sweet	87
MACDONNELL, In re	122
Mackalley's Case	45
Mahon v. Justice	9, 126, 127
Main v. McCarty	79, 80
Malcolmson v. Gibbons	46
v. Scott	128
Mangold v. Thorpe	56
Marsh v. Smith	78
Marshall v. Critico	151
Marshelsea, The	21
Matthews v. State	100
May v. Shumway	155
Mayhew v. Parker	59
Mayor of Norwich v. Berry	152
McCandless v. State	74
McCarthy v. De Armitt	69, 78
McCourt v. People	99, 102
McCracken v. Ansley	41, 43
McCullough v. Com.	82
McDuffie v. Beddoe	64

TABLE OF CASES

[References are to pages.]

McGough v. Wellington	24	Newell v. Whigham	23
McKay v. Ray	158	New Orleans v. U. S.	13
McKenzie v. Gibson	69	Nichols v. Nichols	24
McKnight, Ex parte	126	v. Thomas	164
McLennon v. Richardson	82, 90	North v. People	106
McMahan v. Green	163, 170, 171		
McManus, Ex parte	30, 37	OCEAN STEAMSHIP CO.	
McNeil, Ex parte	152, 155	v. Williams	59
McNeil, The Case of Archibald	155	O'Connor v. Backlin	117
McQueen v. State	55	Olmstead v. Raymond	54
Mead v. Haws	25, 26	O'Malia v. Wentworth	27
Meek v. Pierce	15, 36	O'Neil v. State	147
Merritt v. Openheim	65	Osborn v. Com.	143
Mesmer v. Com.	106, 109	Oystead v. Shed	91, 92, 95, 172
Mex. Cent. Ry. v. Pinkney	9		
Meyer v. State	162	PADFIELD v. Cabell	31
Middleton v. Price	23	Paetz v. Dain	87
Miers v. State	51	Painter v. People	139
Miles, In re	126, 127	Papineau v. Bacon	169
Miller v. Foley	26, 28	Parris v. Com.	138
Millett v. Baker	14, 31, 58	Parsons v. Lloyd	22
Missouri, etc. R. Co. v. Warner	59	Pastor v. Regan	59
Mitchell v. Lemon	85	Patterson v. State	106, 109
v. State	171	Paul v. Vankirk	27, 36
v. Tibbetts	12	Payson v. Macomber	163
Mix v. People	9	Pearce v. Atwood	19, 30
Mockabee v. Com.	51, 109, 145	People v. Adams	17
Mohr's Case	131	v. Ah Teung	52
Money v. Leach	25	v. Barker	143, 144
Montgomery Co. v. Robinson	39	v. Bartz	74, 76, 80
Moore v. State	146	v. Bemmerly	136
Morrill, Ex parte	77	v. Burt	77, 78
Morton v. Skinner	128	v. Campbell	27, 152
Mosely v. State	55	v. Carlton	106
Mowry v. Chase	41	v. Chase	146
Mullen v. Brown	164	v. Cowteral	96
Mundini v. State	75	v. Cross	126
Murdock v. Ripley	106, 109	v. Curtis	121, 136
Murphy v. People	4	v. Davis	145
Muscoe v. Com.	4, 59, 77	v. Donahue	121
Myall v. Wright	65	v. Duck	139
		v. Dupree	96
NEAGLE, In re	112	v. Durfee	106
Neal v. Joyner	69, 77	v. Gelabert	143
Nelson v. State	11	v. Godfrey	13
Neufeld v. Rodeminski	164	v. Haley	51

TABLE OF CASES

[References are to pages.]

People v. Harrington	116	Poulk v. Slocum	19
v. Haug	79	Powers, In re	78
v. Hennessey	133	v. Russell	133
v. Hockstim	69, 78	Pratt v. Hill	59
v. Husband	148	Prell v. McDonald	33
v. Johnson	75, 76	Pressley v. State	101
v. Kerrigan	5	Price v. Seeley	71
v. McCoy	118, 119	Pruitt v. Miller	170
v. McCrea	139	Purrington v. Loring	24
v. McLaughlin	137	Puryear v. Com.	145
v. McLean	30, 37		
v. Mead	28	QUEEN v. Downey & Jones	18, 28
v. Miller	141		
v. Moore	30, 47, 49, 50	Quinn v. Heisel	80
v. Morehouse	71		
v. Murray	4, 5	RADFORD v. State	146
v. Nolan	102	Rafferty v. People	7, 24, 57
v. Olmstead	145	Ramsey v. State	80, 106, 109
v. Palmer	133	Randall v. State	53
v. Payment	9	Rawlins v. Ellis	46, 153
v. Pichette	134	Read v. Case	86, 90
v. Plath	133	Reed v. Rice	15, 171
v. Pool	51, 78	Regan v. N. Y. etc. R. R. Co.	87
v. Pratt	75	Reggel, Ex parte	128
v. Rose	11	Reg. v. Brown	171
v. Rowe	9	v. Bird	101
v. Sanford	146	v. Downey	18, 28
v. Shanley	29, 30	v. Ingham	4
v. Tarbox	133	v. Rowton	137
v. Townsend	144	v. Smith	145
v. Trull	71	Reid v. Ham	126
v. Van Dam	138	Reifsnyder v. Lee	117
v. Walker	141	Reneau v. State	85, 106, 107, 108
v. Warren	20	Respublica v. De Longchamps	150
v. Weaver	146	Ressler v. Peats	31, 81
v. Wilson	47, 50	Reuck v. McGregor	69
v. Young	141	Rex v. Backhouse	102
Phillips v. Fadden	63, 115, 170	v. Brice	100
Pigman v. State	141	v. Burdette	133
Pike v. Hanson	162	v. Carroll	141
Pinkerton v. Verberg	75	v. Drummond	145, 146
Pitt v. Webley	46	v. Hall	148
Plasters v. State	47	v. Hyams	100
Pond v. People	96	v. James	28
Popejoy, In re	81	v. Kendall	15
Porter v. Swindle	60	v. O'Donnell	118

TABLE OF CASES

[References are to pages.]

Rex v. Osmer	58	Shafer v. Mumma	75
v. Pike	146	Shanley v. Wells	71, 78, 84, 89, 135
v. Pitman	141	Shannahan v. Com.	140
v. Smith	82	Shannon v. Jones	40, 41
v. Smithies	139	Shattuck v. State	53
v. Spriggs	99, 101	Sheldon v. Hill	19
v. Turner	96	In re	123
v. Walker	83	Shields v. State	17
v. Warickshall	144	Ship Richmond v. U. S.	9
v. Weir	28, 36	Shorland v. Govett	23, 172
Reynolds v. Orvis	27	Short v. Symmes	136
v. People	13	Shovlin v. Com.	51, 106
Rickers v. Simcox	117	Siegel v. Connor	69
Rimmer v. Green	152	Simmerman v. State	69
Rischer v. Meehan	107	Simmons v. Vandyke	59
Roberts v. Reilly	130	Simons v. People	146
Robinson, In re	9	Sims v. State	100
v. People	143	Skidmore v. State	106
v. State	44	Slanson, Ex parte	127
Rockwell v. Murray	82	Slomer v. People	164
Roderick v. Whitson	79	Smith v. Clark	29
Rohan v. Sawin	59	v. Jones	154
Rosen v. Fischel	19	v. State	140
Rowan v. State	4	Smythe v. Banks	157
Russell v. State	80	So. P. R. Co. v. Johnson	139
Russen v. Lucas	43	Spalding v. Preston	117
Rutland Bank v. Barker	158	Spies v. Illinois	15
		Sprigg v. Stump	34
SACO v. Wentworth	4	Staff, In re	5
Salisbury v. Com.	69	Stalcup v. State	137
Sanborn v. Carleton	37	Stanley, Ex parte	121
Sandow v. Jarvis	92	Starchman v. State	17
Sarah Way, In re	75	Starr v. Com.	145
Savage v. State	145	v. U. S.	31, 48
Schwabacher v. People	98, 141	State v. Aaron	145
Scircle v. Neeves	59, 60	v. Adams	145
Scott v. Eldridge	78	v. Ah Chuey	119
Ex parte	9	v. Ah Lee	146
v. People	145	v. Albee	5
v. State	98	v. Anderson	46, 109
Searles v. Viets	41, 43	v. Archibald	72
Secor v. Bell	151	v. Atkinson	17
Sedgebeer v. Moore	64	v. Baldwin	146
Semayne's Case	90, 93	v. Bates	55
Sewell v. State	139	v. Beebe	52
Shadgett v. Clipson	27	v. Belk	51, 112

xviii TABLE OF CASES
[References are to pages.]

State v. Bland	105, 109	State v. Glover	126
v. Boon	98, 99, 100	v. Graham	119, 144
v. Bradford	143	v. Grant	77
v. Bradneck	139	v. Griswold	16
v. Brewster	9	v. Groning	99
v. Brown	53, 143	v. Guy	79
v. Bryant	106, 107	v. Hall	126, 130
v. Buck	155	v. Harvey	133
v. Caldwell	47, 49	v. Hecox	99
v. Campbell	71	v. Henry	99, 103
v. Cantieny	57	v. Holmes	148
v. Carmen	5	v. Hooker	52
v. Chee Gong	134	v. Hudson	128
v. Chrisp	76	v. Hull	137
v. Conners	99	v. Hunter	53, 170
v. Craine	146	v. Hutchinson	143
v. Creson	137	v. James	4, 56
v. Curtis	47, 50	v. Jenkins	97
v. Daniel	146	v. Jones	28, 52
v. Davidson	133	v. Kaub	17
v. Davis	5, 53	v. Kaufman	5
v. Day	9, 143	v. Kealy	9, 126
v. Deniston	171	v. Keggon	136
v. Dennis	52	v. Kelly	13
v. Dierberger	106, 107, 135	v. Killett	33, 34
v. Dietz	106, 108	v. Komstell	143
v. Donohoo	138	v. Kring	116
v. Dooley	46	v. Lafferty	76, 82, 106, 109
v. Drake	58	v. Lapage	137, 138
v. Dula	47, 49, 50	v. Leach	52
v. Edwards	17, 139	v. Lewis	54
v. Eliott	146	v. Mahon	86, 106, 107, 109
v. Estis	52	v. Mann	34
v. Fair	137	v. McAfee	80
v. Fiske	141	v. McDonald	19
v. Flanagan	73	v. McGee	137
v. Flynn	17	v. McKinney	139
v. Fowler	145	v. Miller	47, 106
v. Frederic	139	v. Miner	140
v. Freeman	52, 59, 60, 76	v. Mooring	90
v. Fuller	106, 109	v. Morgan	69
v. Garrand	145	v. Mowry	68
v. Garrett	50, 52, 119	v. Nutting	12
v. Garvey	141	v. O'Brien	99
v. Gay	47	v. Oliver	90
v. German	133	v. Parker	169

TABLE OF CASES

[References are to pages.]

State v. Pate	106		State v. Weber	95
v. Patterson	9		v. Wenzell	27
v. Pearce	145		v. West	78, 140
v. Phelps	143		v. White	73, 137
v. Phinney	46, 47, 48		v. Williams	80, 95, 97
v. Pomeroy	17		v. Wilson	146
v. Potts	97		v. Woods	100
v. Powell	100		v. Worden	5
v. Pugh	110		Stedman v. Crane	94, 96
v. Reed	145, 146		Steenerson v. Polk Co. Com'rs	39, 47
v. Reid	99			
v. Richter	130		Stephens v. Wilkins	7, 11, 19, 20
v. Ritchie	53		Stetson v. Packer	7, 11, 28
v. Rodman	139		Stevenson v. Smith	65, 158
v. Rogers	132		Stewart v. State	138
v. Rose	51		Stone v. Carter	66
v. Ross & Mann	9		Stuart v. Harris	117
v. Russell	79		Stutsman Co. v. Wallace	168
v. Schleagel	138		Sullivan v. State	145
v. Schlottman	75		Sultan, In re	130
v. Schuermann	74		Sumner v. Beeler	21
v. Shaw	90		Sutton v. Allison	66
v. Shelton	46, 136, 145		Swart v. Kimball	5
v. Sigman	85, 106		Swift v. Chamberlain	152, 157
v. Simmons	9			
v. Smith	9, 10, 89, 134		TAAFE v. Kyne	73
v. Somnier	146		v. Slevin	172
v. Sorrel	136		Tackett v. State	31
v. Spaulding	47, 49		Tallemon v. Cardenas	158
v. Stalcup	112, 116, 171		Tarleton v. Fisher	22
v. Stancill	50		Tarvers v. State	46
v. Stewart	126		Tate v. State	61
v. Stouderman	82		Taylor v. Porter	4
v. Stuth	75		v. Taintor	86
v. Symes	77		Teagarden v. Graham	69
v. Tatro	140, 143		Tefft v. Ashbaugh	11
v. Taylor	77, 134		Tellefson v. Fee	19, 21
v. Tice	145		Thomas v. Kinkead	85, 107
v. Townsend	47, 49, 50		Thompson v. State	147
v. Vanderpool	125		Thompson's Case	155
v. Van Tassel	17		Thurston v. Adams	19
v. Walker	140		v. Martin	21
v. Wamire	54		Tickner v. People	99
v. Ward	36, 37, 138		Tillman v. Beard	79
v. Warner	72		Timmons v. State	100
v. Warren	95		Tiner v. State	107, 108

TABLE OF CASES

[References are to pages.]

Tooley's Case	77	Wade v. Chaffee	77
Topeka v. Heitman	72	Wahl v. Walton	83
Towns v. State	134	Wakely v. Hart	69
Tracy v. Seamans	41	Walker v. State	98, 99, 100
v. Williams	33, 78	Walters v. State	134
Trask v. People	17	Ward v. State	139
Tremblay v. Graham	65	Ware v. Leveridge	74
Trustees v. Schroeder	4	Warner v. Grace	78
Tubbs v. Tukey	23, 29, 63	v. Riddiford	41
Turner, In re	152	v. State	141
Twilley v. Perkins	59	Warren v. Kelley	21
Tyson, In re	64	Wartner v State	5
		Watson v. Bodell	21
Union Depot etc. Co.		v. State	170, 171
v. Smith	79	v. Watson	23
United States v. Anthony	147, 168	Webb v. State	29
v. Bannister	64	Welby v. Beard	153
v. Benner	44, 151	Wells v. Jackson	30
v. Bevans	13	Welsh v. Wilson	97
v. Boyd	69	Wentworth v. People	52
v. Brooks	75	West v. Cabell	26, 28, 56
v. Clark	85, 107	Westervelt v. Gregg	4
v. Dickerman	12	Wheelock v. Archer	172
v. Faw	90	White v. Edmunds	111
v. Fullheart	106	Ex parte	129
v. Hart	76, 153	In re	123, 138
v. Jailer	47, 49	v. Kent	79
v. Kirby	153	v. State	140, 144, 146
v. Lafontaine	150	v. Vallely	130, 131
v. Ortiga	151	Whitehead v. Keyes	24, 44, 67
v. Raucher	120, 125	Whittaker v. State	146
v. Rice	47, 49, 50	Wiggins v. Norton	59
v. Taylor	5	Wilcox v. Nolze	131
v. Watts	125	Willard v. State	133
		Williams v. Com.	144
Vanderpool v. State	164	v. Jones	42
Van Straaten v. People	140	v. People	133, 136
Vaughn v. Com.	146	v. Spencer	94
v. Scade	6	v. State	5, 17, 45, 57, 77, 78, 106, 107, 109
Veneman v. Jones	79	v. Tidball	26
Vincent, Ex parte	98	Wills v. Jordan	78
v. Stinehour	167	v. State	13
Virginia, Ex parte	4	Wilmarth v. Burt	22, 56, 152, 163
Von Der Ahe, In re	86	Wilson v. Barnhill	66
Voorhees, In re	130	Ex parte	70

TABLE OF CASES

[References are to pages.]

Wilson v. State	69, 70	Woolfolk v. State	118
v. Tucker	30	Work v. State	5
v. United States	139	Wrexford v. Smith	69
Wiltshire v. Lloyd	152	Wright v. Com.	68, 78
Wiltze v. Holt	60	v. Court	112, 116
Winkler v. State	27	v. Keith	45, 56
Winslow v. State	133	v. State	107, 137
Wise v. Withers	7, 11	Wroe v. State	145
Wolf v. State	51		
Wood v. Graves	163	YATES v. People	49
v. Neale	155	Young v. Com.	137
v. Ross	27		

THE LAW OF ARREST

CHAPTER I

THE RIGHT OF PERSONAL LIBERTY

§ 1. **Definition.** — The right of personal liberty consists in the power of locomotion, of changing situation, or moving one's person to whatsoever place one's own inclination may direct, without imprisonment or restraint, unless by due course of law.[1]

§ 2. **A Natural Right.** — This right is a natural one such as has ever been the birthright of every freeman, even in those ages before civilization had exercised its softening influence upon man's passions, and is now guarded with jealous care by that inexorable mistress, " the law of the land."

§ 3. **Secured by Magna Charta.** — It is a right which was stoutly maintained by our English ancestors, and is one of the rights which they secured to themselves by the famous Magna Charta (Great

---

[1] 1 Blackstone's Commentaries, 135.

Charter), which was given to the barons of England by King John, in 1215, under persuasion of the sword.

The right of personal liberty as reduced to written evidence by this great charter was not a new law, but was rather a correction of abuses of the right, which then endangered the liberty of the English people. The language of the Magna Charta is, that no freeman shall be taken or imprisoned but by the lawful judgment of his equals, or by the law of the land.

§ 4. **Strengthened by "Petition of Right" and "Habeas Corpus Act."** — By the Petition of Right in 1628, it was further enacted that no freeman should be imprisoned or detained without cause shown, to which he might make answer according to law.

Following this legislative enactment came the act of 1664, by which any one restrained of his liberty by order or decree of any illegal court, or even by the command of the king himself in person, or by warrant of the council board, or of any of the privy council, should have, upon demand of his counsel, a writ of *habeas corpus* (you may have the body) to bring his body before the court of king's bench, or common pleas, who should determine whether the cause of his commitment be just, and thereupon do justice to the party accused. And by the act of 1679, commonly known as the " Habeas

Corpus Act," the methods of obtaining this writ were plainly pointed out.

§ 5. **English Bill of Rights. — Excessive Bail Prohibited.** — To guard against the evasion of this act it was further enacted in the English Bill of Rights, in 1689, that excessive bail should not be required.

§ 6. **American Bill of Rights. — Due Process of Law.** — This right of immunity from illegal restraint was brought to the American shores by our forefathers and became a part of the common law of this country. Subsequently it was incorporated into the American Bill of Rights, — as embraced in the first ten amendments to the Constitution of the United States, — by the adoption of the fifth amendment, which provides that no person shall be deprived of his liberty without due process of law. And a similar provision exists in all the State constitutions.[2]

Due process of law means that whatever the legal proceeding may be, it must be enforced by public authority, whether sanctioned by age or

[2] Article 12 of the Bill of Rights in the Constitution of Massachusetts, which was enacted about seven years before Amendment 5 of the Constitution of the United States was adopted, declares "no subject shall be arrested, imprisoned, despoiled, or deprived of his property, immunities, or privileges, put out of the protection of the law, exiled or deprived of his life, liberty, or estate, but by the judgment of his peers, or the law of the land." This Bill of Rights was fashioned from Magna Charta.

custom, or newly devised in the discretion of the legislative power, in furtherance of the general public good, which regards and preserves the principles of liberty and justice.[3] It means that neither life, liberty, nor property can be taken, nor the enjoyment thereof impaired, except in the course of the regular administration of the law in the established tribunals.[4] Therefore an arrest without a warrant, where one is required by law, is not due process of law.[5]

Relating to the higher crimes, due process of law is said to denote a lawful indictment or presentment of good and lawful men,[6] and a public trial by jury,[7]

---

[3] Hurtado v. California, 110 U. S. 516; Rowan v. State, 30 Wis. 129; King v. Berchet, 1 Show. (Eng. K. B.) 106; Reg. v. Ingham, 5 B. & S. (Eng. Q. B.) 257; Westervelt v. Gregg, 12 N. Y. 202; Bank of Columbia v. Okely, 4 Wheat. (U. S.) 235; Brown v. Levee Commissioners, 50 Miss. 468; Davidson v. New Orleans, 96 U. S. 97.

[4] Ex parte Virginia, 100 U. S. 366.

[5] Muscoe v. Com., 86 Va. 443; State v. James, 78 N. C. 455; Trustees v. Schroeder, 58 Ill. 353.

[6] Coke, 2d Inst. 50; affirmed in Jones v. Robbins, 8 Gray (Mass.), 329, in which see dissenting opinion by Justice MERRICK; disaffirmed in Hurtado v. California, supra cit., in which see dissenting opinion by Justice HARLAN. See also Taylor v. Porter, 4 Hill (N. Y.), 140; Hoke v. Henderson, 4 Dev. (N. C.) 1; Jones v. Perry, 10 Yerger (Tenn.), 59; 3 Story on Const. U. S. 661; 2 Kent's Com. 13; Saco v. Wentworth, 37 Me. 172; Emerick v. Harris, 1 Binn. (Pa.) 416; Murphy v. People, 2 Cow. (N. Y.) 815; Jackson v. Wood, 2 Conn. 819; Beers v. Beers, 4 Conn. 535.

[7] People v. Murray, 89 Mich. 276.

before a court of competent jurisdiction. Therefore, where the court at the trial of one charged with murder, directed an officer to stand at the door of the court-room " and see that the room is not overcrowded, but that all respectable citizens be admitted, and have an opportunity to get in when they shall apply," it was held that the right of the accused to a public trial, guaranteed to him by the constitution, had been violated.[8]

§ 7. **Constitutional Right cannot be Waived.** — As a general rule the accused, at least in a felony case, cannot waive his constitutional right to a trial by a jury of twelve men; and it is the duty of courts to see that the constitutional rights of a defendant in a criminal case shall not be violated.[9] And the fact that the defendant was negligent in raising his objections is not material.[10]

---

[8] People v. Murray, 89 Mich. 276.

[9] Hill v. People, 16 Mich. 351; Canceini v. People, 18 N. Y. 128; Work v. State, 2 Ohio St. 296; United States v. Taylor, 3 McCrary (U. S. C. C.), 500; Harris v. People, 128 Ill. 589; Brown v. State, 8 Blackf. (Ind.) 561; League v. State, 36 Md. 257; Allen v. State, 54 Ind. 461; Wartner v. State, 102 Ind. 51; Swart v. Kimball, 43 Mich. 443; State v. Carman, 63 Iowa, 130; Bond v. State, 17 Ark. 290; State v. Davis, 66 Mo. 684; Bell v. State, 44 Ala. 393; Williams v. State, 12 Ohio St. 622; Kleinschmidt v. Dunphy, 1 Mont. 118. *Contra:* State v. Worden, 46 Conn. 349; Hallinger v. Davis, 146 U. S. 314; In re Staff, 63 Wis. 285; State v. Kaufman, 51 Iowa, 578; People v. Kerrigan, 73 Cal. 222; State v. Albee, 61 N. H. 423.

[10] Hill v. People, 16 Mich. 351.

In courts not of record, however, as in justices' courts, a trial by less than twelve men is legal.[11]

The provisions in Article III, Constitution of the United States, respecting the trial of crimes by jury, relates to the judicial power of the United States alone, and does not apply to State courts.[12]

§ 8. **Personal Liberty demands Restraint.** — The assurance of personal liberty does not license any person to be free from restraint; on the contrary, it demands such necessary restraint of persons as will insure the utmost amount of personal liberty to each, for the safety and well-being of society are paramount to individual liberty.

§ 9. **The Limit of Governmental Control.** — The government has the right to control its subjects up to that point where society is safe, but it has no right to go beyond the point of safety.[13] Any law which restrains a man from doing mischief to his fellow-man increases the personal liberty of mankind, but every wanton and causeless restraint of the will of the subject is a degree of tyranny.[14]

§ 10. **Rights of Subjects are Equal.** — It is one of the most commendable features of our republican

[11] Vaughn *v.* Scade, 30 Mo. 600; Hill *v.* People, 16 Mich. 351.
[12] Eilenbecker *v.* Plymouth Co., 134 U. S. 31; Edwards *v.* Elliott, 21 Wall. (U. S.) 557.
[13] Petition of Ferrier, 103 Ill. 373.
[14] 1 Bl. Com. 126.

form of government that our laws are equal, just, and impartial, and that the humblest member of society has rights and remedies for the infraction of those rights, that are not exceeded by the rights or remedies of any other man, no matter how high his station. No officer of the law can, with impunity, set those rights at defiance. All officers of the government, from the highest to the lowest, are creatures of the law, and are bound to obey it.

§ 11. **Rights must be Respected.** — It is, therefore, removed from the whim or ignorance of any magistrate to issue, or of any person to serve any legal process whatever unless the provisions of law be strictly followed; and any restraint of a person, except by due process of law, amounts to a false imprisonment, for which both magistrate and officer may be liable in damages to the person deprived of his liberty, and the imprisonment may also be made the subject of a criminal prosecution.[15]

[15] Fisher v. McGirr, 1 Gray (Mass.), 45; Stetson v. Packer, 7 Cush. (Mass.) 564; Stephens v. Wilkins, 6 Pa. St. 260; Emery v. Hapgood, 7 Gray (Mass.), 55; Rafferty v. People, 69 Ill. 111; Gurney v. Tufts, 37 Me. 130; Wise v. Withers, 3 Cranch (U. S.), 337; Entick v. Carrington, 2 Wils. (Eng. C. P.) 275; Groome v. Forrester, 5 M. & S. (Eng. K. B.) 314; Allen v. Gray, 11 Conn. 95.

CHAPTER II

THE ISSUANCE AND SERVICE OF LEGAL PROCESS

Process.

§ 12. **Definition.** — Process is a writ, warrant, subpoena, or other formal writing issued by authority of law; also the means of accomplishing an end, including judicial proceedings.[1]

The word "process" is also used as a general term to cover all the written means of compelling a defendant to appear in court, whether in a civil or in a criminal action.

§ 13. **Statutes abrogate the Common Law.** — Any process issued according to the rules of the common law, and any act done under precedent of the weight of authority as laid down in the judicial decisions will be valid, and will justify all persons acting therein, unless the authority of such common law and judicial precedents has been abrogated by constitutional legislative enactments; for where the common law and the statutes are in conflict, the latter always control.

[1] Gollobitsch *v.* Rainbow, 84 Iowa, 567.

JURISDICTION.

§ 14. Procured by Stratagem or Fraud. — No court can, at common law, exercise jurisdiction over a party in a civil case unless he is served with process within the territorial jurisdiction of the court or voluntarily appears.[2] But a person cannot claim immunity, in a criminal case, because he was enticed into the jurisdiction by stratagem and fraud,[3] except in case of an extradition under a treaty, it being well established that when a prisoner is before a court, legally charged with a crime for which he is to be tried, the court will not be obliged to inquire how he came there; and the want of authority for a prisoner's arrest cannot protect him from prosecution.[4] So where

---

[2] Mex. Cent. Ry. v. Pinkney, 149 U. S. 194; Kendall v. United States, 12 Pet. (U. S.) 524; Harris v. Hardeman, 14 How. (U. S) 334.

[3] Ex parte Brown, 28 Fed. Rep. (U. S.) 653; In re Doo Woon, 18 Fed. Rep. (U. S.) 898.

[4] Dow's Case, 18 Pa. St. 37; Com. v. Wait, 131 Mass. 417; Ex parte Scott, 9 B. & C. (Eng. K. B.) 446; Lopez & Sattlers' Case, 1 Dearsly & Bell's C. C. (Eng.) 525; State v. Smith, 1 Bailey (S. C.), 283; State v. Brewster, 7 Vt. 118; In re Durant, 60 Vt. 176; State v. Patterson, 116 Mo. 505; State v. Day, 58 Iowa, 678; State v. Ross & Mann, 21 Iowa, 467; State v. Kealy, 89 Iowa, 94; Ship Richmond v. U. S., 9 Cranch (U. S.), 102; Mahon v. Justice, 127 U. S. 700; Ker v. People, 110 Ill. 627; Mix v. People, 26 Ill. 34; People v. Payment, 109 Mich. 553; Ex parte Barker, 87 Ala. 4; Lagrave's Case, 14 Abb. Pr. N. S. (N. Y.) 333, note; People v. Rowe, 4 Parker Cr. (N. Y.) 253. *Contra:* In re Robinson, 29 Neb. 135; State v. Simmons, 39 Kan. 262.

an embezzler was kidnapped from Peru and brought forcibly to the United States, without the existing treaty powers having been invoked, although an ample treaty of extradition existed between that country and the United States, the State court may proceed to try the offender, and the United States courts can give him no relief.[5]

And where a felon convict, after being sentenced to be executed for stealing a slave, was pardoned, upon the condition that he immediately leave the State and never return, he afterward violated the condition by returning to the State wherein he was pardoned; whereupon the governor of that State offered a reward for his capture. He fled from that State to an adjoining State, whence he was forcibly taken without process and brought back to the State where the crime was committed, and his motion for a discharge from arrest was refused.[6]

§ 15. **Procured by Illegal Arrest.** — Where a party is taken from his own house for drunkenness to answer to a complaint for that offence, which had been duly made and received, it is immaterial upon the question of his guilt and punishment therefor, whether he had been arrested legally or illegally, or arrested at all before the complaint was made.[7]

[5] Ker *v.* Illinois, 119 U. S. 436.
[6] State *v.* Smith, 1 Bailey (S. C.), 283.
[7] Com. *v.* Conlin, 184 Mass. 195.

§ 16. **Effect of Want of Jurisdiction.** — If the magistrate issuing the process has no jurisdiction of the subject-matter, the process is not merely voidable but wholly void, and an officer acting under it is a trespasser,[8] as is also the magistrate who issues it,[9] and the party making the complaint.[10]

And an unconstitutional statute, purporting to give jurisdiction, will not justify either magistrate or officer.[11] But lack of jurisdiction of the person will not invalidate the process if the defect does not appear on its face.[12]

§ 17. **Finding Prisoner Guilty of Lesser Offence than that Charged.** — If an offender is lawfully before a court charged with an offence of which the court has jurisdiction, he may, upon trial, be found guilty of a lesser offence which is a degree of the greater crime, or relates to the same transaction, if it is charged in a separate count, of which the court otherwise would have no jurisdiction.[13]

---

[8] Fisher v. McGirr, 1 Gray (Mass.), 45; Wise v. Withers, 3 Cranch (U. S.), 337; Entick v. Carrington, 2 Wils. (Eng. C. P.) 275.

[9] Stetson v. Packer, 7 Cush. (Mass) 564.

[10] Stephens v. Wilkins, 6 Pa. St. 260; Emery v. Hapgood, 7 Gray (Mass.), 55.

[11] Fisher v. McGirr, supra cit.

[12] Tefft v. Ashbaugh, 13 Ill. 602; Clarke v. May, 2 Gray (Mass.), 410.

[13] People v. Rose, 15 N. Y. Suppl. 815. But see Nelson v. State, 10 Humph. (Tenn.) 518.

Although if the lesser crime were charged as a separate offence the court would not have jurisdiction.

But where the greater and lesser offence are contained in the same count, a court may not convict of the lesser crime which is not within its jurisdiction.[14]

§ 18. **Foreign Vessels.** — A foreign merchant ship coming within our harbors is subject to our local jurisdiction the same as any foreign private person.[15] But over a public ship, such as a man-of-war, a State court in whose port the ship is can never have jurisdiction.

§ 19. **Ceded Territory.** — Over a locality ceded by a State to the United States, the jurisdiction of the courts of the ceding State does not extend, except by a special reservation in the ceding act; and a reservation in such act, of concurrent jurisdiction to serve in the ceded locality any civil or criminal State processes, does not take from the United States its *exclusive* legislative and judicial authority; and an offence therein committed is triable in the United States courts alone.[16]

The federal courts also have exclusive jurisdiction over crimes committed within parts of a State ceded for the purpose of arsenals, dockyards, forts,

---

[14] State *v.* Nutting, 16 Vt. 261.

[15] U. S. *v.* Dickerman, 92 U. S. 520.

[16] Mitchell *v.* Tibbetts, 17 Pick. (Mass.) 298, referring to the Charlestown navy yard.

magazines, postoffices, and all other public buildings of the United States.[17]

So a State court has no jurisdiction of murder in a fort ceded to the government.[18]

ARREST.

§ 20. **Modes of making.** — An arrest may be made in four ways: 1. By warrant; 2. By an officer without warrant; 3. By a private person also without warrant; 4. By a hue and cry.[19]

When the offender is not likely to abscond before a warrant can be obtained, it is in general better to apprehend him by a warrant than for a private person or officer to arrest him of his own accord, because if the justice should grant his warrant erroneously, no action lies against the party obtaining it.[20]

WARRANTS.

§ 21. **Search Warrant.** — **Definition.** — A search warrant is a warrant requiring the officer to whom it is addressed to search a house, or other place,[21]

---

[17] U. S. v. Bevans, 3 Wheat. (U. S.) 386; New Orleans v. U. S., 10 Pet. (U. S.) 711; Clay v. State, 4 Kan. 54; Wills v. State, 3 Heisk. (Tenn.) 142; Reynolds v. People, 1 Col. 180; People v. Godfrey, 17 Johns. (N. Y.) 230.

[18] State v. Kelly, 76 Me. 331.

[19] 4 Bl. Com. 290.

[20] Leigh v. Webb, 3 Esp. (Eng. N. P.) 166.

[21] In California it has been held that a search warrant may be issued to search a person. Collins v. Lean, 68 Cal. 284.

therein specified,[22] for property therein alleged to have been stolen, and if the same shall be found upon such search, to bring the goods so found, together with the body of the person occupying the same, who is named, before the justice or other officer granting the warrant, or some other justice of the peace, or other lawfully authorized officer.[23]

§ 22. **Procedure in Issuing.** — It issues on a complaint, made on oath or affirmation, by the suspecting party, and the complainant should aver that the property has been stolen, and that he has cause to suspect, and does suspect, that it is secreted in the house or place proposed to be searched,[24] which place must be described, and no place other than that described can be searched. Nor can any property other than that described be seized.

A search warrant will issue either to recover stolen property or procure evidence of a crime. In California it may be issued against a person.[25] Like other warrants, it should be signed, and, when required by statute,[26] sealed by the magistrate issuing

[22] Com. v. Lucy, 150 Mass. 164.
[23] Bouvier's Law Dict. (Search **Warrant**); Grumon v. Raymond, 1 Conn. 40.
[24] Com. v. Phillips, 16 Pick. (Mass.) 214; Grumon v. Raymond, supra cit.
[25] Collins v. Lean, 68 Cal. 284.
[26] Millett v. Baker, 42 Barb. (N. Y.) 215.

THE ISSUANCE AND SERVICE OF LEGAL PROCESS 15

it. It may be directed either to an officer, or, in case of necessity, to a private person.[27]

§ 23. **Constitutional Provisions.** — The Constitution of the United States, Article IV, Amendment, provides, "The right of the people to be secure in their persons, houses, papers, and effects against unreasonable searches and seizures, shall not be violated, and no warrant shall issue but on probable cause, supported by oath or affirmation, and particularly describing the place to be searched and the persons or things to be seized." But this provision does not apply to searches and seizures made under direction of State authorities.[28] Provisions, however, similar to that enacted in the Constitution of the United States, have been enacted in the various State constitutions,[29] and thereby afford the citizens of the particular State ample protection against unreasonable searches and seizures.

§ 24. **Permission will justify Searching without a Warrant.** — The constitutional provisions respecting search warrants apply only to cases where the search is without the consent of the occupant of the

---

[27] Meek v. Pierce, 19 Wis. 318; Com. v. Foster, 1 Mass. 493; 4 Bl. Com. 291; 1 Hale's Pleas of Crown, 581; 2 Hawkins' Pleas of Crown, c. 13, § 28; Rex v. Kendall, 1 Ld. Raym. (Eng. K. B.) 66; Kelsey v. Parmalee, 15 Conn. 265; Blatcher v. Kemp, 1 H. Black. (Eng. C. P.) 15.

[28] Spies v. Illinois, 123 U. S. 131; Reed v. Rice, 2 J. J. Marshall (Ky.), 44.

[29] See Const. Mass., Part I., Art. XIV.

premises, therefore where permission is given to search, either by the occupant or his agent, a search warrant is not necessary. So where, after the arrest of one on a charge of arson, police officers went to his place of business in the burned building, and without a search warrant, but with the permission and assistance of his agent, who was in charge of the premises, found and removed certain articles which were used as evidence against the accused at the trial, the introduction of this evidence could not be objected to as having been taken in violation of the State constitution regulating searches and seizures, or that it compelled him to give evidence against himself, because the accused was bound by the consent given by his agent, and in consequence there was no " seizure " or compulsion.[30]

§ 24 a. **Illegal Seizure does not destroy Admissibility of Evidence obtained Thereby.** — Where papers which are pertinent to the issue are illegally taken from the possession of the party against whom they are offered as evidence, the fact of the illegal seizure cannot be offered as a valid objection to their admissibility, because the court limits the inquiry to the competency of the proffered testimony and will not stop to inquire as to the means by which the evidence was obtained.[31]

[30] State v. Griswold, 67 Conn. 290.
[31] Adams v. New York, 192 U. S. 585 ; Com. v. Dana, 2 Metc. (Mass.) 329; State v. Griswold, 67 Conn. 306.

And where a police officer, armed with a search warrant calling for a search for intoxicating liquors upon the premises of the defendant's husband, took two letters which he found at the time, it was held that a trespasser may testify to pertinent facts observed by him, or may put in evidence pertinent articles or papers found by him while trespassing, and although he may be held responsible civilly or criminally for the trespass, his testimony is not thereby rendered incompetent.[32]

§ 25. **Purposes for which a Search Warrant will Issue.** — The purposes for which a search warrant will issue are usually fully described by statute,[33] and generally embrace the search for stolen property, intoxicating liquors, gaming implements, counterfeit money, and instruments used in making it, and other articles made, sold, or kept in violation of law.

§ 26. **Bench Warrant. — Definition.** — A bench warrant is a process issued by a judge from the

---

[32] Com. v. Tibbetts, 157 Mass. 519. See also Com. v. Acton, 165 Mass. 11; Com. v. Smith, 166 Mass. 370; Chastaug v. State, 83 Ala. 29; State v. Flynn, 36 N. H. 64; State v. Edwards, 51 W. Va. 220; Shields v. State, 104 Ala. 35; Bacon v. United States, 97 Fed. Rep. 35; State v. Atkinson, 40 S. C. 363; Williams v. State, 100 Ga. 511; State v. Pomeroy, 130 Mo. 489; Guidrat v. People, 138 Ill. 103; Trask v. People, 151 Ill. 523; Starchman v. State, 62 Ark. 538; People v. Adams, 85 N. Y. App. 390; State v. Van Tassel, 103 Iowa, 6; State v. Kaub, 15 Mo. App. 433; Legatt v. Tollervey, 14 East (Eng. K. B.), 302.

[33] See Revised Laws of Mass. c. 217, §§ 1-8.

bench, that is, by the court itself, for the arrest of a person, either in a case of contempt of court, or after an indictment has been found, or to bring in a witness who has not obeyed the subpœna. It requires all the formalities of other warrants of arrest.

The only purpose of the term " bench warrant " is to distinguish it from a warrant issued by a magistrate, who may be a judge not sitting officially, or a justice of the peace, whereas a bench warrant is always issued by a judge at an official sitting. It is the usual warrant to issue after an indictment has been found.

A bench warrant is bad which does not direct that the party shall be brought before some judge or justice.[34]

§ 27. **Warrant of Arrest. — Definition.** — A warrant of arrest is a legal process issued by competent legal authority, directing the arrest of a certain person, or persons, upon sufficient grounds, which must be stated in the warrant.[35]

§ 28. **Issuing Magistrate need not have Trial Jurisdiction.** — A warrant is usually issued by a magistrate having jurisdiction to try the offence, but a justice of the peace who has no jurisdiction to try an offence may act in a ministerial capacity,

[34] Queen v. Downey & Jones, 7 Q. B. (Eng.) 281.
[35] Drennan v. People, 10 Mich. 169.

THE ISSUANCE AND SERVICE OF LEGAL PROCESS 19

and issue a warrant returnable before a court which has the necessary trial jurisdiction.[36]

§ 29. **What Executing Officer must know.** — An officer called upon to execute a warrant is charged with two duties which he must observe in order to insure his own freedom from liability. He must know (1) that the magistrate, or court who issues the warrant has general jurisdiction of the subject-matter,[37] and (2) that the warrant is valid upon its face.[38]

§ 30. **How far a Warrant Valid upon its Face protects the Officer.** — From the decisions it does not seem clear as to just how far an officer is protected by a warrant that is valid upon its face.

One line of cases seems to hold that, on the ground of public policy, and in order to secure

[36] Com. v. Roark, 8 Cush. (Mass.) 210. See also Gold v. Bissell, 1 Wend. (N. Y.) 217.
[37] State v. McDonald, 3 Dev. (N. C.) 471; Allen v. Gray, 11 Conn. 95; Tellefson v. Fee, 168 Mass. 188; Stephens v. Wilkins, 6 Pa. St. 260; Earl v. Camp, 16 Wend. (N. Y.) 562; Ela v. Shepard, 32 N. H. 277; Hines v. Chambers, 29 Minn. 7; Hann v. Lloyd, 21 Vroom (N. J.), 1. *Contra:* Emery v. Hapgood, 7 Gray (Mass.), 55.
[38] Emery v. Hapgood, supra cit.; Clark v. Woods, 2 Exch. (Eng.) 395; Pearce v. Atwood, 13 Mass. 324; Eames v. Johnson, 4 Allen (Mass.), 382; Thurston v. Adams, 41 Me. 419; Brown v. Howard, 86 Me. 342; Rosen v. Fischel, 44 Conn. 371; Frazier v. Turner, 76 Wis. 562; Sheldon v. Hill, 33 Mich. 171; Poulk v. Slocum, 3 Blackf. (Ind.) 421.

prompt and effective service of legal process, officers, and those acting under them, need only to look upon the warrant, and if that is fair and valid upon its face, showing no defect or want of jurisdiction, the officer may justify under it, although it is wholly void,[39] and that he need not take notice of extrinsic facts.[40]

While another line of reasoning, which seems to be the weight of authority, is that a warrant is void upon its face if the whole proceeding in which it was issued was beyond the jurisdiction of the issuing court, and that if the officer knows the facts in the case he is conclusively presumed to know the law, and therefore liable.

So where a justice of the peace issued a warrant for the collection of road taxes, not having jurisdiction over such taxes, the officer was held liable for executing the warrant.[41] And where, by treaty of 1827 between the United States and Sweden and Norway,[42] exclusive jurisdiction in an action for wages brought by a Norwegian sailor against the captain of a Norwegian vessel was given to the Norwegian consul of the particular port in which the vessel was lying, the courts of the United States have no jurisdiction; and an officer who serves a warrant issued by a municipal court after these

---

[39] Emery *v.* Hapgood, 7 Gray (Mass.), 58.
[40] People *v.* Warren, 5 Hill (N. Y.), 440.
[41] Stephens *v.* Wilkins, 6 Pa. St. 260.
[42] 8 U. S. Stats. 346, 352.

facts have been brought to his attention, is liable, although the want of jurisdiction is not apparent on the face of the warrant, which is in proper form.[43]

If the process is void upon its face, it is no protection whatever, and the officer or other party who serves it is liable civilly and criminally. If he kills in the act of serving the process, it is murder.

§ 31. Ignorance of the Law is no Excuse. — If either the jurisdiction or warrant is faulty, the fact that the officer does not know the law governing these matters will not excuse him,[44] because every one is conclusively presumed to know the law, the well-settled maxim of the law being, "Ignorance of the law excuses no one."

§ 32. Ignorance of Fact may Excuse. — But although ignorance of the law is no excuse, ignorance of fact may be a valid excuse; and if the officer is ignorant of jurisdictional facts, which

---

[43] Tellefson v. Fee, 168 Mass. 188. See also Warren v. Kelley, 80 Me. 512; Batchelder v. Currier, 45 N. H. 460; Campbell v. Sherman, 35 Wis. 103; Leachman v. Dougherty, 81 Ill. 324.

[44] Sandford v. Nichols, 13 Mass. 286; Fisher v. McGirr, 1 Gray (Mass.), 1, 45; Warren v. Kelley, 80 Me. 512; Batchelder v. Currier, 45 N. H. 460; Thurston v. Martin, 5 Mason (U. S. C. C.), 497; Campbell v. Sherman, 35 Wis. 103; Sumner v. Beeler, 50 Ind. 341; The Marshalsea, 10 Rep. (Eng. K. B.) 68 b; Crepps v. Durden, Cowp. (Eng. K. B.) 640; Watson v. Bodell, 14 M. & W. (Eng. Exch.) 57.

ignorance is not attributable to his own negligence, he may justify by a process that is fair and valid upon its face.

§ 33. **Officer must serve Void Warrant if the Defect is not on its Face.** — On the other hand, if the warrant is void, for any cause other than want of jurisdiction, and the officer knows it, he is protected in serving it if the defect does not appear on its face;[45] and he has no right to refuse to serve a warrant, issued by a court of competent jurisdiction, if it is valid on its face, even though it be void.[46]

If there is an insufficiency in the complaint, the officer is not liable if the defect does not appear on the face of the warrant,[47] because he has the right to rely upon the warrant alone.[48]

A clerical mistake in copying the facts from the complaint, at least in the matter of a date, does not make the warrant invalid, if it is not misleading.[49]

[45] Kennedy v. Dunclee, 1 Gray (Mass), 65; Parsons v. Loyd, 3 Wils. (Eng. C. P.) 345; Gasset v. Howard, 10 Ad. & El. N. s. (Eng. Q. B.) 454; Allison v. Rheam, 3 S. & R. (Pa.) 139.

[46] Wilmarth v. Burt, 7 Metc. (Mass.) 257; Tarlton v. Fisher, 2 Doug. (Eng. K. B.) 671; Cameron v. Lightfoot, 2 W. Bl. (Eng. K. B.) 1190.

[47] Donahue v. Shed, 8 Metc. (Mass.) 326; Com. v. Murray, 2 Va. Cases, 504.

[48] Wilmarth v. Burt, supra cit.

[49] Heckman v. Swartz, 64 Wis. 48.

§ 34. **Return of Warrant is Necessary to its Validity.** — But even though a warrant be issued by a court of competent jurisdiction over both party and subject-matter, and though the warrant be fair and valid upon its face, it is of no protection whatever to the officer if he does not return it to court after he serves it.[50]

§ 35. **Life of a Warrant.** — A warrant remains in force until it is returned; even if the accused has been arrested and escapes, he may be taken again on the same warrant, if it has not been returned. After its return, however, it has no validity; nor can it be altered,[51] for its life is then extinct.

§ 36. **Effect of the Return.** — The effect of the return by the officer is that, as against himself,[52] it is conclusive proof of the service and of the other facts which it recites, while as against the parties, it is at least *prima facie* proof,[53] and in most States

---

[50] Brock *v.* Stimson, 108 Mass. 520; Tubbs *v.* Tukey, 3 Cush. (Mass.) 438; Dehm *v.* Hinman, 56 Conn. 320. See also Com. *v.* Tobin, 108 Mass. 426; Shorland *v.* Govett, 5 B. & C. (Eng. K. B.) 485; Middleton *v.* Price, 1 Wils. (Eng. C. P.) 17.

[51] Com. *v.* Roark, 8 Cush. (Mass.) 210.

[52] Blue *v.* Com., 2 J. J. Marshall (Ky.), 26; Benjamin *v.* Hathaway, 3 Conn. 528; Hensley *v.* Rose, 76 Ala. 373.

[53] Watson *v.* Watson, 6 Conn. 334; Newell *v.* Whigham, 102 N. Y. 20.

it is conclusive proof against the parties also.[54] In an action against a public officer his return is *prima facie* but not conclusive evidence in his favor, although it is conclusive in the suit in which it is made.[55] Nor is a return of a rescue on a writ conclusive evidence in behalf of the officer in an action brought against him for the escape of a prisoner.[56]

An officer will not be permitted to introduce evidence to show that although he has omitted to mention in his return that he has done things which he should have done, he has nevertheless done them.[57] And he will not be allowed to contradict his own return for his own benefit.[58]

The return, by permission of the court, may be amended by the officer.[59]

§ 37. **Warrants in Blank are Void.** — A warrant must not be issued in blank with view of later writing in the name of the defendant.[60] Such warrants are absolutely void.

[54] Nichols v. Nichols, 96 Ind. 433; Green v. Kindy, 43 Mich. 279.
[55] McGough v. Wellington, 6 Allen (Mass.), 505.
[56] Whitehead v. Keyes, 3 Allen (Mass.), 495; Barrett v. Copeland, 18 Vt. 67.
[57] Grant v. Shaw, 1 Root (Conn.), 526.
[58] Purrington v. Loring, 7 Mass. 388; Gardner v. Hosmer, 6 Mass. 324.
[59] Johnson v. Stewart, 11 Gray (Mass.), 181; Lake's Case, 15 R. I. 628; Dwiggins v. Cook, 71 Ind. 579.
[60] Rafferty v. People, 69 Ill. 111.

§ 38. **General Warrants are Void.** — Nor can a warrant be legally issued in a general way against any one of a certain class of persons;[61] but a statute may authorize the arrest, without warrant, of any one of a certain class, as, for example, vagrants, prostitutes, etc.[62]

§ 39. **Warrant must particularly describe the Party to be arrested.** — A warrant may be valid although it does not contain the name of the person whose arrest is directed. But for want of the true name of such person there must be such sufficient description of him in the warrant that he may be identified therefrom; as, for example, stating his occupation, his personal appearance, and peculiarities, the place of his residence, or other circumstances of identification.

§ 40. **Officer must rely on Name alone.** — Where a warrant gives a fictitious name, without stating that the name is fictitious, and that the true name is unknown, and follows with a description of the person, the officer must rely on the name alone, and cannot justify the arrest of a party whose name is other than that appearing in the warrant, even though he is the party described and intended. As where a warrant was issued against "John Doe, the person carrying off the cannon," the arrest of Levi

---

[61] Com. v. Crotty, 10 Allen (Mass.), 403; Mead v. Haws, 7 Cow. (N. Y.) 332.

[62] Money v. Leach, 3 Burrows (Eng. K. B.), 1766.

Mead is not justifiable, although he was taken in the act of carrying off the cannon, and was the person intended.[63]

§ 41. **General Warrants are prohibited.** — If the description in a warrant is so general that it may be applied to different persons, it is open to the objection that it is a general warrant,[64] and is for that reason in violation of the Constitution of the United States, Article IV, Amendment, which requires a particular description of a person to be seized,[65] and any person whose arrest is attempted thereunder is justified in resisting such unlawful arrest.

§ 42. **Never Sufficient that Intended Party was arrested.** — It is never sufficient that the party intended to be arrested was the one actually apprehended. The warrant must so describe the party arrested that he may know whether he is bound to submit. So where the complaint was against "John R. Miller," and the warrant commanded the arrest of "the said William Miller," the officer was not justified in arresting John R. Miller, although it was proved that he was the person intended.[66]

[63] Mead v. Haws, 7 Cowen (N. Y.), 332; West v. Cabell, 153 U. S. 78; Harris v. McReynolds, 10 Col. App. 532. *Contra:* by statute in Arizona: Williams v. Tidball, 2 Ariz. (1885).

[64] Com. v. Crotty, 10 Allen (Mass.), 404.

[65] West v. Cabell, 153 U. S. 78.

[66] Miller v. Foley, 28 Barb. (N. Y.) 630. See also Griswold v. Sedgwick, 6 Cowen (N. Y.), 455.

§ 43. **Party known by two Names may be arrested by either.** — But where a person is known by two names, and equally well by either, a warrant may command his arrest under either name, even though it be the wrong one.[67]

§ 44. **No Protection to Officer who serves a Warrant without Authority.** — An officer cannot be protected by a warrant that is not issued to himself to serve, nor is he protected unless he has authority to serve it.[68]

§ 45. **The Requisites of a Valid Warrant.** — It is somewhat difficult to say just what are the requisites of a valid warrant, but in a general way it may be said that a warrant must have all the requisites demanded by the constitutional and statutory provisions of the particular State in which it is issued; it must show on its face that it was issued by a magistrate having jurisdiction of both party and subject-matter;[69] and here it may be noted that where the magistrate has no jurisdiction, it cannot be conferred by the consent of the party defendant.[70]

---

[67] Shadgett v. Clipson, 8 East (Eng. K. B.), 328; Cole v. Hindson, 6 T. R. (Eng.) 234.

[68] Reynolds v. Orvis, 7 Cowen (N. Y.), 269; Wood v. Ross, 11 Mass. 271; Paul v. Vankirk, 6 Binn. (Pa.) 123; State v. Wenzel, 77 Ind. 428; O'Malia v. Wentworth, 65 Me. 129; Winkler v. State, 32 Ark. 539.

[69] In re Bonner, 151 U. S. 242; Reynolds v. Orvis, supra cit.; Fisher v. Shattuck, 17 Pick. (Mass.) 252.

[70] People v. Campbell, 4 Parker Cr. Rep. (N. Y.) 386.

It must state the offence with which the party is charged, which must be an offence against the law,[71] and that the necessary complaint on oath or affirmation was made.[72] It must show the time of issuance,[73] and the authority to issue.[74] It must correctly name the defendant, or so accurately describe him that from the description he may be identified.[75] It must be directed to the proper officer, either by name, or by a description of the office which he holds.[76] It must *command* the arrest,[77] and not leave it optional with the officer to arrest or not as he may choose; and command the officer to bring the defendant before some authorized magistrate.[78]

A warrant should bear the signature of the justice who issues it, contain all the statutory requirements,

---

[71] People v. Mead, 92 N. Y. 415; Johnson v. State, 73 Ala. 21; State v. Jones, 88 N. C. 671.

[72] Caudle v. Seymour, 1 Q. B. (Eng.) 889; Grumon v. Raymond, 1 Conn. 40.

[73] Donahoe v. Shed, 8 Metc. (Mass.) 326.

[74] Com. v. Ward, 4 Mass. 497; Halstead v. Brice, 13 Mo. 171.

[75] Com. v. Crotty, 10 Allen (Mass.), 403; West v. Cabell, 153 U. S. 78; Miller v. Foley, 28 Barb. (N. Y.) 630.

[76] Rex v. Weir, 1 Barn. & Cres. (Eng. K. B.) 288; Com. v. Foster, 1 Mass. 493; Com. v. Moran, 107 Mass. 239.

[77] Abbott v. Booth, 51 Barb. (N. Y.) 546.

[78] Stetson v. Packer, 7 Cush. (Mass.) 562; Com. v. Wilcox, 1 Cush. (Mass.) 503; Reg. v. Downey, 7 Q. B. (Eng.) 281; Bookhout v. State, 66 Wis. 415.

THE ISSUANCE AND SERVICE OF LEGAL PROCESS 29

which generally include a seal,[79] and be dated. It should contain a command to the officer to make a return thereof and his doings thereon. But the want of such command does not excuse him from the obligation of making a proper return.[80]

§ 46. **Warrant must be in Possession of Officer.** — The officer or private person making an arrest with a warrant, in a case where a warrant is necessary,[81] must have the warrant in his possession at the time of making the arrest;[82] and it is immaterial whether the person taken has demanded an inspection of the warrant, for it is the legal right of the person arrested that such shall be the situation, and therefore where the situation does not exist, the arrest is a legal wrong.[83]

The fact that the arrested party knows that a warrant has been issued will not relieve the arresting party of the necessity of having the war-

---

[79] In Massachusetts, it is provided that justices and special justices of police, district, and municipal courts may issue warrants under their own hands and *seals*. Rev. Laws of Mass. c. 160, § 35. A trial justice, however (not having an official seal), may issue a warrant under his hand alone. Rev. Laws of Mass. c. 216, § 3.

[80] Tubbs *v.* Tukey, 3 Cush. (Mass.) 438.

[81] People *v.* Shanley, 40 Hun (N. Y.), 477; Codd *v.* Cabe, 13 Cox C. C. (Eng.) 202.

[82] Webb *v.* State, 51 N. J. Law, 189; Smith *v.* Clark, 53 N. J. Law, 197. But see Cabell *v.* Arnold, 86 Tex. 102.

[83] Smith *v.* Clark, supra cit.

iant with him.[84] And there is no such thing as *constructive* possession of a warrant.[85]

But where a sheriff is armed with a warrant, his deputy may make an arrest within the sight or hearing of the superior officer, although the warrant is not actually in his possession.[86]

§ 47. **Warrants may issue on Sunday.** — In absence of statute, a warrant may be issued on Sunday,[87] but no arrest, except in cases of treason, felony, or breach of the peace, can be made on Sunday.[88]

§ 48. **Authority to alter a Warrant.** — No person, other than the issuing magistrate, has the right to alter a warrant,[89] because if altered by a third party it would not be the warrant issued by the magistrate who signed it.

§ 49. **Arrest in Different County.** — In absence of statutory authority, no arrest can be made in one county in a State, on a warrant issued by a justice of the peace or judge of another county in that

---

[84] People *v.* Shanley, 40 Hun (N. Y.), 477.

[85] Ibid.

[86] People *v.* McLean, 68 Mich. 480; Kirbie *v.* State, 5 Tex. App. 60; Ex parte McManus, 32 New Brunswick, 481; Com. *v.* Black, 12 Pa. Co. Ct. 31; People *v.* Moore, 2 Doug. (Mich.) 1.

[87] Pearce *v.* Atwood, 13 Mass. 347.

[88] Wilson *v.* Tucker, 1 Salk. (Eng. K. B.) 78; Stat. 29, Car. II. c. 7.

[89] Haskins *v.* Young, 2 Dev. & B. (N. C.) 527; Wells *v.* Jackson, 3 Munf. (Va.) 458.

State, unless the warrant is indorsed by a justice of the peace or judge of the county in which the arrest is made.[90]

§ 50. **Warrant may be Valid without a Seal.** — A warrant ought to be under the hand and seal of the justice, but it seems sufficient if it be in writing and signed by him, unless a seal is expressly required by statute.[91]

The warrant of a commissioner of the United States is not void for lack of a seal, because such commissioner has no official seal and is not required by statute to affix one to warrants issued by him.[92]

---

[90] Jones v. State, 26 Tex. App. 1; Ressler v. Peats, 86 Ill. 275; Copeland v. Islay, 2 Dev. & Bat. (N. C.) 505; Ledbetter v. State, 23 Tex. App. 247; 4 Bl. Com. 291.

In Massachusetts, if the defendant escape from, or is out of the county in which the warrant is issued, the officer may pursue and take him in any county in the Commonwealth, as if in his own county. Rev. Laws, c. 217, § 28.

[91] Padfield v. Cabell, Willes Rep. (Eng. Com. Pl.) 411. A warrant of arrest is valid if it has the signature of the magistrate; the seal is no longer necessary. Burley v. Griffith, 8 Leigh (Va.), 442. *Contra:* Tackett v. State, 3 Yerger (Tenn.), 392. At common law, a seal was not necessary to a warrant issued by a justice of the peace, and is only made so, even in criminal cases, when specifically required by statute. Millett v. Baker, 42 Barb. (N. Y.) 215. "We are of the opinion that there was no settled rule at common law invalidating warrants not under seal, unless the magistrate issuing the warrant had a seal of office, or a seal was required by statute." Chief Justice FULLER, in Starr v. U. S., 153 U. S. 619.

[92] Starr v. U. S., 153 U. S. 614.

CHAPTER III

WHO MAY ISSUE A WARRANT

§ 51. Mandamus may compel Justice to Act. — A justice before whom a complaint is laid, is bound to take some direct action on the facts laid in the complaint, and if he refuse to consider the facts, or what is of the same effect, if he decline to issue the warrant because of some reason not disclosed by the evidence before him, a mandamus will lie to compel the justice to take some action on the facts before him. But the limit of the writ of mandamus will be to compel action, and not to dictate what that action shall be.[1]

§ 52. Constitutional Provision. — It is prescribed by the Constitution of the United States, Article IV, Amendment, that no warrant shall issue "except upon probable cause supported by oath or affirmation," and the constitutions of the several States have similar provisions.[2]

The Complaint.

§ 53. Who may make Complaint. — It is usually provided by statute that any person having knowl-

---

[1] 15 Eng. Rul. Cases, 127; Hempstead Co. *v.* Graves, 44 Ark. 317.

[2] See Const. of Mass. Part I., Art. XIV.

edge of the commission of an offence for which a warrant may lawfully issue, may make a written complaint, subscribed by him, together with the required oath or affirmation before the proper officer, whereupon the warrant may issue.[3] When an arrest is made without a warrant, the arresting party should, upon delivering his prisoner to the proper authority, immediately make a complaint setting forth the offence for which the arrest was made. Without the complaint the court would not have jurisdiction to try or dispose of the cause.[4]

§ 54. **Not necessarily made in Writing.** — Unless required by statute, the complaint need not be in writing.[5]

§ 55. **Who may issue Warrants.** — The statutes of the particular State in which the arrest is to be made usually designate the officers who have powers to issue warrants of arrest.[6]

In Massachusetts, a justice or special justice of a district court may receive complaints and issue warrants when the court is not in session; and it is to be presumed that the justice acted within the

[3] Rev. Laws of Mass. c. 217, § 22.

[4] Tracy v. Williams, 4 Conn. 107; Bingham v. State, 59 Miss. 530; Prell v. McDonald, 7 Kan. 426.

[5] State v. Killett, 2 Bailey (S. C.), 289.

[6] In Massachusetts, warrants may be issued by justices of the supreme judicial court, of the superior court, or of the police, district, or municipal courts, and trial justices. Rev. Laws of Mass. c. 217, § 21.

authority given him, and that the court was not in session when the warrant was issued.[7]

§ 56. **Warrant issued without Complaint is Illegal.** — It is the duty of the magistrate before issuing a warrant to require evidence on oath amounting to a direct charge, or creating a strong suspicion of guilt.[8] A warrant issued upon common rumor and report of the guilt of the accused, though it recites that there was danger of his escaping before witnesses could be summoned to enable the judge to issue it upon oath, is illegal, and the officer was justified in refusing to serve it,[9] because it was void upon its face.

§ 57. **Constitutional Provisions.** — There being some doubt whether the common law absolutely required that a warrant should issue only upon information on oath, the clause concerning probable cause on oath was added to the fourth amendment to the Constitution of the United States. The legal effect of this provision of the Constitution is that process of any kind for the arrest of a person on a criminal charge is void, unless issued upon sufficient information under oath, and an arrest thereon is unlawful.[10]

[7] Com. v. Lynn, 154 Mass. 405.
[8] Com. v. Phillips, 16 Pick. (Mass.) 214; State v. Mann, 5 Ired. (N. C.) 45.
[9] Connor v. Com., 3 Binn. (Pa.) 38.
[10] Sprigg v. Stump, 8 Fed. Rep. (U. S.) 207. *Contra:* State v. Killett, 2 Bailey (S. C.), 289.

§ 58. **"Subscribed" means "Written Beneath."** — When the statute requires that a complaint shall be "subscribed," that is, written beneath, it is not sufficient that the signature of the complainant be placed below the description of the goods stolen, and above the charge of larceny,[11] for, said the court in this case, "Such looseness and carelessness in instituting criminal proceedings are not to be encouraged."

§ 59. **Statutory Jurisdiction implies Power to Arrest.** — Where a statute gives a justice jurisdiction over an offence, it impliedly gives him power to apprehend any person charged with such offence, and especially after a party has neglected a summons.[12]

In any proceeding of a criminal nature, and brought in the name of the commonwealth, a justice has authority to proceed by a warrant of arrest or a summons at his discretion. The power of arrest is laid down to attend all offences which justices of the peace have authority, by statute, to punish. It is necessary to prevent the escape of transient and irresponsible persons, and yet should be exercised with caution and moderation.[13]

§ 60. **Warrant directed to a Private Person.** — It has been decided that warrants may be directed

[11] Com. v. Barhight, 9 Gray (Mass.), 113.
[12] Bane v. Methuen, 2 Bing. (Eng. Com. Pl.) 63.
[13] Com. v. Borden, 61 Pa. St. 272.

to private persons as well as officers,[14] but a warrant may be directed to a private person only in case of necessity, and when that necessity is expressed in the warrant.[15] A private person cannot deputize another to serve a warrant directed to him, although he may demand assistance.

§ 61. **Warrant directed to Officer.** — Warrants may be directed to officers either by their particular names, or by the description of their office; and it has been decided that in the first case the officer may execute the warrant anywhere within the jurisdiction of the magistrate who issued it; in the latter case not beyond the precincts of his office. And where a warrant of a magistrate was directed, "To the constables of W. and to all other his majesty's officers," it was held that the constables of W., their names not being inserted in the warrant, could not execute it out of the district.[16]

§ 62. **Delegating Authority to serve Process.** — An officer to whom process is directed may deputize another to serve the process within his presence, that is, within the sight or hearing of the superior

---

[14] Dehm v. Hinman, 56 Conn. 320; Doughty v. State, 33 Tex. 1; State v. Ward, 5 Harr. (Del.) 496; Dietrichs v. Schaw, 43 Ind. 175; Hayden v. Songer, 56 Ind. 42.

[15] Com. v. Foster, 1 Mass. 493; Meek v. Pierce, 19 Wis. 318.

[16] Rex v. Weir, 1 Barn. & Cres. (Eng. K. B.) 288; Paul v. Vankirk, 6 Binn. (Pa.) 123.

officer who has possession of the warrant,[17] but the deputized party cannot re-delegate his authority.[18]

ARREST FOR CONTEMPT.

§ 63. **Contempt of Legislative Body.** — A legislative body, when acting in a judicial capacity, has authority to issue a warrant for the arrest of such persons as are guilty of contempt of that body; but a sergeant-at-arms of the United States, to whom a warrant is directed, has no authority to appoint a deputy to execute that warrant outside of a place where the United States has exclusive jurisdiction.[19]

§ 64. **Contempt of Court.** — When a judge, in the legitimate exercise of his jurisdiction, is defiantly disobeyed, he may commit the offender instantly to prison for contempt of court; and where a judge of a superior court, acting within his jurisdiction, commits for contempt, he is not bound in the warrant (if a warrant is made out) to set forth particularly the ground of the commitment.[20]

---

[17] People v. McLean, 68 Mich. 480; Kirbie v. State, 5 Tex. App. 60; Ex parte McManus, 32 New Brunswick, 481; Bowling v. Com., 7 Ky. L. Rep. 821; Com. v. Black. 12 Pa. Co. Ct. 31; Com. v. Field, 13 Mass. 321; State v. Ward, 5 Harr. (Del.) 496. See § 75, infra.

[18] State v. Ward, supra cit.

[19] Sanborn v. Carleton, 15 Gray (Mass.), 399.

[20] 15 Eng. Rul. Cases, 1.

If the contempt is in the face of the court no warrant is necessary; an order is sufficient.[21]

If a justice of the peace has power to commit for contempt, it must be by a warrant in writing, for a time certain;[22] but a judge of a superior court may commit for an uncertain time.

[21] Holcomb v. Cornish, 8 Coun. 374.
[22] Rex v. James, 5 Barn. & Ald. (Eng. K. B.) 894.

CHAPTER IV

WHAT CONSTITUTES AN ARREST[1]

§ 65. Definition. — To arrest is to deprive a person of his liberty by legal authority. It is the seizing a person and detaining him in the custody of the law.[2]

§ 66. Requisites of a Legal Arrest. — To constitute a legal arrest it is necessary that the arresting party have lawful authority, and exercise that authority in a lawful place, and at a lawful time, and that the arrested party be not exempt from arrest.

To complete an arrest there must be a taking into custody, either by touching the defendant for the purpose of arresting him, which purpose must be brought to the knowledge of the defendant, or by his submission to words of arrest with the knowledge that he is being arrested.[3]

---

[1] See also "False Imprisonment," § 271 et seq.

[2] Bouvier's Law Dictionary (Arrest). Montgomery County v. Robinson, 85 Ill. 174 [quoting Bouvier's Law Dict.]. "Apprehension" is more properly used in criminal cases; "arrest" in civil cases. Hogan v. Stophlet, 179 Ill. 150.

[3] Steenerson v. Polk Co. Com'rs, 68 Minn. 509.

§ 67. **Reading Warrant is not Sufficient.** — Merely reading the warrant to the accused does not make an arrest.[4] But where an officer went to the accused with a warrant, and finding her sick in bed, read it to her, and told her that if she did not give a bond he " would haul her to jail," it was held that there was an arrest, although he did not touch her or exercise any physical control over her.[5]

§ 68. **Importance of Consummation of the Arrest.** — The completion of the acts which constitute an arrest becomes very important in certain cases, for until this act of taking into custody is consummated, there can be neither a criminal rescue of the prisoner, nor a criminal escape by him. And an action of false imprisonment will not lie against the arresting party until all the acts necessary to a legal arrest have been consummated.

In an action for false imprisonment the following facts appeared: An officer having a warrant for the arrest of the plaintiff and two of his sons, met the plaintiff and one of his sons in a wagon. The officer said: " I have a warrant for you and your two sons." The plaintiff asked: " What for?" The officer replied: " For stealing pumpkins." The plaintiff started to get out of the wagon, when the officer said: " You can go home and get your

[4] Baldwin v. Murphy, 82 Ill. 485; George v. Radford, 3 C. & P. (Eng. N. P.) 464.
[5] Shannon v. Jones, 76 Tex. 141.

horses put up and take your tea, and come down."
The plaintiff went home, and with his two sons
went to the house of the officer, and called out:
"Here's your prisoners."

The officer said: "You move on and I will overtake you." They went on. The officer overtook them as they got to the house of the justice, and they went in together. *Held*, that the evidence showed an arrest of the plaintiff.[6]

§ 69. **Touching the Accused is not Necessary.** — In making an arrest it is not necessary that the party making the arrest shall even touch the person of the arrested party, but it is enough if the arrested party is in the power of the party making the arrest, and submits to the arrest,[7] with the knowledge that he is being arrested.[8]

§ 70. **Understanding of the Parties is Important.** — In construing the acts relied upon to establish the arrest, the intent and understanding of the

---

[6] Searles *v.* Viets, 2 Thomp. & C. (N. Y.) 224.

[7] Mowry *v.* Chase, 100 Mass. 79; Gold *v.* Bissell, 1 Wend. (N. Y) 210; Ahern *v.* Collins, 39 Mo. 145; Alderich *v.* Humphrey, 29 Ont. 427; Warner *v.* Riddiford, 4 C. B. N. S. (Eng.) 180; Searles *v.* Viets, 2 Thomp. & C. (N. Y.) 224; Tracy *v.* Seamans, 7 N. Y. St. 144; Journey *v.* Sharpe, 49 N. C. 165; Brushaber *v.* Stegemann, 22 Mich. 266; Shannon *v.* Jones, 76 Tex. 141; Courtoy *v.* Dozier, 20 Ga. 369; Field *v.* Ireland, 21 Ala. 240; McCracken *v.* Ansley, 4 Stroh. (S. C.) 1.

[8] Jones *v.* Jones, 13 Ired. (N. C.) 448.

parties become very important; and whether the parties understood the acts to amount to an arrest is a question of fact for the jury.[9]

§ 71. **Complete Control is Sufficient.** — If an officer assumes control over the person of the defendant, as where when in a room with the accused he locks the door, and tells him that he is a prisoner, there no submission or touching is necessary, for the defendant has been completely taken into the custody of the law.[10]

§ 72. **Avoiding Custody by Accepting Alternative.** — Where the accused, to avoid being taken into custody, accepts an alternative which is offered him by the arresting party, there the arrest is complete, although no physical control is exercised. As where an officer came to the room of the party whose arrest was sought, and finding him ill in bed, told him that unless he deliver a certain article or find bail, he must either take him or leave a man with him, and the party complied with his order, it was held a sufficient arrest.[11]

But where an officer stated to the defendant that he had a capias for him, and the defendant asked for a couple of days to procure a bond, to which the officer assented, and upon receiving the bond two

---

[9] Jones *v.* Jones, 13 Ired. (N. C.) 448.
[10] Williams *v.* Jones, Cas. temp. Hard. (Eng. K. B.) 298.
[11] Grainger *v.* Hill, 4 Bing. N. C. (Eng. C. P.) 212.

days later, indorsed the arrest on the capias as of that date, it was held that there was no arrest prior to giving the bond.[12]

§ 73. **Bare Words not Sufficient to Arrest.** — Bare words alone will not make an arrest, if the defendant resists the arrest.[13] In such case there must be an actual touching of the person of the defendant in order that the arrest be effective,[14] and in all cases there must be a restraint of the person, — a taking into custody.[15]

So where a salesman, upon suspicion that a person had stolen goods from his employer's store, touched the suspected person on the shoulder and requested her to return to the store, which she did, it was held there was no arrest, there being no restraint or compulsion exercised.[16]

And where an officer had a warrant against the accused, and went upon his premises, saying, "I arrest you," the accused with a fork in his hand prevented the officer touching him, and retreated from the officer's presence, it was held not to be an arrest, because there was no submission or restraint.[17]

[12] McCracken v. Ansley, 4 Strob. (S. C.) 1.
[13] Searles v. Viets, 2 Thomp. & C. (N. Y.) 224; Hill v. Taylor, 50 Mich. 549; Conoly v. State, 2 Tex. App. 412; Russen v. Lucas, 1 C. & P. (Eng. N. P.) 153.
[14] Genner v. Sparks, 1 Salk. (Eng. K. B.) 79.
[15] French v. Bancroft, 1 Metc. (Mass.) 502; Kernan v. State, 11 Ind. 471.
[16] Hershey v. O'Neill, 36 Fed. Rep. (U. S) 168.
[17] Genner v. Sparks, 1 Salk. (Eng. K. B.) 79.

§ 74. **Touching consummates Arrest, though Accused takes Immediate Flight.** — An officer effects an arrest of a person whom he has authority to arrest, by laying his hand on him for the purpose of arresting him, though he may not succeed in stopping and holding him.[18]

§ 75. **Arresting Hand may be of Officer's Assistant.** — And it is not necessary that the arresting hand be the officer's own hand, but may be that of an assistant, even though the officer is not actually in sight; yet when an arrest is made by his assistant or follower, the officer ought to be so near as to be considered as acting in it.[19]

A private person who is a member of a sheriff's posse may make a legal arrest, though the sheriff is at a considerable distance away, provided he is within the county proceeding about the business of the arrest, because he is then constructively present.[20]

And the question in these cases does not turn on the fact of distance, so long as the officer is within his territory, and is *bona fide* and strictly engaged in the business of the arrest. So where an officer having a warrant to apprehend several persons who had riotously assembled and when in endeavoring

[18] Whitehead *v.* Keyes, 3 Allen (Mass.), 495; U. S. *v.* Benner, Bald. (U. S. C. C.) 239.

[19] Emery *v.* Chesley, 18 N. H. 198; Whitehead *v.* Keyes, supra cit.

[20] Robinson *v.* State, 93 Ga. 77.

to serve his process he was resisted, and, being unable to make the arrest, commanded several persons to assist him and guard the house while he went to the next town, about four miles distant, to get a sufficient force to enable him to execute the warrant, it was held that the officer was *constructively* present, and that during his temporary absence for the purpose of getting further assistance, those whom he had commanded to assist him, and who by that command were bound to assist him, were liable to punishment for permitting or assisting the offenders to escape.[21]

§ 76. **Time of Arrest.** — A person may be apprehended on a criminal charge at any time, in the night as well as in the day,[22] and it lies within the officer's discretion to choose the night instead of the day for the purpose of making an arrest.[23] Though the common law prohibits arrests on Sundays, it excepts the cases of treason, felony, and breach of the peace.[24] " Breach of the peace" is

---

[21] Coyles *v.* Hurtin, 10 Johns. (N. Y.) 85.

[22] Mackalley's Case, 9 Coke (Eng. K. B.), 66; Williams *v.* State, 44 Ala. 41. Respecting arrest after sunset in civil cases, the Massachusetts statute provides, " An arrest shall not be made after sunset, in cases in which a certificate of a magistrate is required, unless it is specially authorized therein for cause." Rev. Laws of Mass. c. 168, § 27.

[23] Wright *v.* Keith, 24 Me. 163.

[24] By Stat. 29 Car. II. c. 7, § 6, "No person upon the Lord's day shall serve or execute, or cause to be served or

held to include all indictable offences,[25] therefore the common law only prohibited arrests in civil cases on Sunday.

§ 77. **Place of Arrest.** — Respecting the place of arrest, it may be said that no place affords protection to offenders against the criminal law. Yet to preserve order and decorum, an arrest could not be made in open court, but should be made after the adjournment of court, or outside the court-room. And even the clergy may, on a criminal charge, be arrested while in their churches,[26] though it is illegal to arrest them in any civil case while in the church to perform divine service, or going to or returning from the same, on any day.[27]

Without a warrant an arrest can only be made in the State wherein the offence was commited.[28]

§ 78. **Officer must make known his Authority.** — A person about to be arrested is entitled to know that he is arrested by lawful authority,[29] and after

executed, any writ, process, warrant, order, judgment, or decree, except in cases of treason, felony, or breach of the peace."

[25] Rawlins *v.* Ellis, 16 Mees. & W. (Eng. Exch.) 172; Keith *v.* Tuttle, 28 Me. 326; Ex parte Levi, 28 Fed. Rep. (U. S.) 651.

[26] Pit *v.* Webley, Cro. Jac. 321; State *v.* Dooley, 121 Mo. 591 ; Ledbetter *v.* State, 23 Tex. App. 247.

[27] Bacon's Abr. Trespass, 23.

[28] State *v.* Shelton, 79 N. C. 605; Tarvers *v.* State, 90 Tenn. 485; Malcolmson *v.* Gibbons, 56 Mich. 459. *Contra:* State *v.* Anderson, 1 Hill (S. C.), 327.

[29] State *v.* Phinney, 42 Me. 384; Com. *v.* Weathers, 7

being apprised of the lawful authority, if he submits to the arrest,[30] he has a right to know the grounds on which he is arrested. But a person resisting arrest is not entitled to see the warrant or know its contents so long as he resists;[31] and whether he resists or not, if he has actual notice of the lawful authority by which he is arrested, the officer is not obliged to show or read his warrant.[32]

§ 79. **Officer need not Imperil his Precept.** — An officer is not required in any case to part with the warrant from his possession, for that is his justification.[33] Nor is he bound to exhibit it when there is reason to apprehend that it will be lost or destroyed; he must, however, in some way inform the

Kulp (Pa.), 1; Kindred *v.* Stitt, 51 Ill. 401; State *v.* Miller, 7 Ohio N. P. 458.

[30] State *v.* Townsend, 5 Harr. (Del.) 487; Lewis *v.* State, 3 Head (Tenn.), 127; Arnold *v.* Steeves, 10 Wend. (N. Y.) 514; State *v.* Curtis, 2 N. C. 543; Plasters *v.* State, 1 Tex. App. 673; State *v.* Miller, 7 Ohio N. P. 458; State *v.* Gay, 18 Mont. 51.

[31] Com. *v.* Cooley, 6 Gray (Mass.) 350; Com. *v.* Hewes, 1 Brewst. (Pa.) 348.

[32] People *v.* Wilson, 55 Mich. 506; see § 81, infra; Com. *v.* Cooley, supra cit.; State *v.* Townsend, 5 Harr. (Del.) 487; Bellows *v.* Shannon, 2 Hill (N. Y.), 86; State *v.* Dula, 100 N. C. 423; People *v.* Moore, 2 Doug. (Mich.) 1; State *v.* Spaulding, 34 Minn. 361; Com. *v.* Hewes, 1 Brewst. (Pa.) 348; State *v.* Caldwell, 2 Tyler (Vt.), 212; U. S. *v.* Jailer, 2 Abb. (U. S.) 265; U. S. *v.* Rice, 1 Hughes (U. S.), 560. *Contra:* Steenerson *v.* Polk Co. Com'rs, 68 Minn. 509.

[33] State *v.* Phinney, 42 Me. 390.

party that he has a warrant, and comes as an officer to execute it, and not as a wrongdoer.[34] But the arresting party is not obliged to show his warrant if the arrest might be lawfully made without a warrant.

§ 80. **Effect of Officer's Failure to exhibit his Authority.** — Where an arrest has been made by a party not known to be an officer, and who refuses, on demand, to exhibit his precept or declare his authority, and resistance is made to such officer, and death ensues to the officer from such resistance, such killing will not be murder, but manslaughter only.[35] And it has been held that the settled rule " where a person having authority to arrest, and using the proper means for that purpose, is resisted, he can repel force with force, and if the party making the resistance is unavoidably killed, the homicide is justifiable," may be invoked by a person who resists and kills the officer, if he was ignorant of the fact that he was an officer.[36]

The only effect of the omission of the officer to declare his authority, or to show his warrant where it is his duty to show it, is to deprive him of the protection which the law throws around its ministers, when in the rightful discharge of their official duty.[37]

[34] Bellows v. Shannon, 2 Hill (N. Y.), 86.
[35] State v. Phinney, 42 Me. 390.
[36] Starr v. United States, 153 U. S. 614.
[37] State v. Phinney, supra cit.

§ 81. **Arrest by Known Officer is Notice of Authority.** — A person is held to know that he is arrested by lawful authority when the arrest is made by an officer, within his own jurisdiction, who is generally known to be an officer.[38] And this knowledge is presumed to exist when the arresting officer is in the uniform of a police officer, or when the officer exhibits the badge of his office.[39]

But the knowledge will not be presumed to exist unless the circumstances are such that the accused may clearly be presumed to know that the party arresting was an officer in uniform. So where the prisoner, on a dark night, was pursued by a mob, which, having severely beaten him, now threatened to kill him for having wounded one of their number in a fight, and one of the pursuers, who was an officer in uniform, being in advance of the others, seizes the prisoner, and the prisoner kills him, it is a justifiable act of self-defence, unless the prisoner knew that the party who had seized him was an officer, which, on account of the existing darkness and other circumstances, was extremely doubtful.[40]

---

[38] Com. v. Cooley, 6 Gray (Mass.), 350; State v. Townsend, 5 Harr. (Del.) 487; U. S. v. Rice, 1 Hughes (U. S.), 560; People v. Moore, 2 Doug. (Mich.) 1; State v. Spaulding, 34 Minn. 361; Bellows v. Shannon, 2 Hill (N. Y.), 86; U. S. v. Jailer, 2 Abb. (U. S.) 265; State v. Caldwell, 2 Tyler (Vt.), 212; State v. Dula, 100 N. C. 423; Com. v. Hewes, 1 Brewst. (Pa.) 348.

[39] Yates v. People, 32 N. Y. 509.

[40] Yates v. People, 32 N. Y. 509.

§ 82. **One not a Known Officer must show his Warrant.** — Any one who is not a known officer acting within the limits of his jurisdiction must exhibit his warrant before making an arrest, if called upon to do so by the party whose arrest is sought, if the warrant is necessary to the arrest.[41] And a special officer must show his warrant *if demanded*, not otherwise.[42]

§ 83. **Actual Notice obviates Necessity of Reading Warrant.** — Actual notice to the arrested party, in any manner, that the arrest is by lawful authority, releases the officer from his duty to show his warrant or read it to the accused.[43]

§ 84. **Strangers not entitled to Notice.** — And in no case is an officer obliged to show his warrant to any person other than the party arrested, nor to him except on request.[44]

§ 85. **Notice may be Constructive.** — Notice of authority to arrest may also be presumed from the

---

[41] People *v.* Moore, 2 Doug. (Mich.) 1; Bates *v.* Com., 13 Ky. L. Rep. 132; State *v.* Stancill, 128 N. C. 606; Frost *v.* Thomas, 24 Wend. (N. Y.) 418; Arnold *v.* Steeves, 10 Wend. (N. Y.) 514; State *v.* Dula, 100 N. C. 423; Cortez *v.* State, 69 S. W. (Tex.) 536; State *v.* Garrett, 60 N. C. 144. But see U. S. *v.* Rice, 1 Hughes (U. S.), 560.

[42] State *v.* Dula, supra cit.; State *v.* Curtis, 2 N. C. 543.

[43] Com. *v.* Cooley, 6 Gray (Mass.), 350; State *v.* Townsend, 5 Harr. (Del) 487; People *v.* Wilson, 55 Mich. 506.

[44] 1 East P. C. 317; 1 Hale's P. C. 458.

circumstances of the case; as where even a private person attempts to arrest one in the act of committing a felony, or where the offender is immediately pursued from the scene of his crime, it is sufficient notice to the party whose arrest is sought.[45]

§ 86. **Resisting Arrest.** — Mere resistance of legal arrest is a crime,[46] because it involves an assault upon the officer; and if the arresting person is killed by the accused or his friends, it is murder.[47] If the resisting person is killed, it is no more than manslaughter, and may be a justifiable homicide.[48] But a person illegally arrested may use such force as is necessary to regain his liberty, and should there be reasonable ground to believe that the officer making the arrest intends shooting the prisoner to prevent his escape, such prisoner may shoot the officer in self-defence.[49] If, however, the person resisting illegal arrest kills merely to prevent the arrest, and not for the purpose of saving himself from serious personal injury, he is guilty of manslaughter, but not of murder.[50]

And whether the arrest be legal or not, the power of arrest may be exercised in such a wanton and

[45] Wolf v. State, 19 Ohio St. 248; Shovlin v. Com., 106 Pa. St. 369; People v. Pool, 27 Cal. 572.
[46] People v. Haley, 48 Mich. 495; State v. Belk, 76 N. C. 10.
[47] Mockabee v. Com., 78 Ky. 380.
[48] State v. Rose, 142 Mo. 418.
[49] Miers v. State, 34 Tex. Cr. Rep. 161.
[50] Com. v. Carey, 12 Cush. (Mass.) 246.

menacing manner as to threaten the accused with loss of life, or some bodily harm. In such a case, though the attempted arrest was lawful, the killing would be justifiable.[51] A charge of resisting an officer cannot be sustained unless the officer resisted was authorized by law to make the arrest at the time and place where the arrest was attempted.[52] If the arrest was by warrant, the process must have been valid on its face, and from a court of competent jurisdiction.[53] It is no defence to a charge of resisting an officer, that the person whose arrest was attempted was not guilty of the offence charged.[54] But where the arrest of the wrong person is attempted, the arrest may be resisted.[55]

§ 87. **After making Arrest. — Officer's Duty.** — It is the officer's duty, upon making an arrest, to keep the prisoner within his custody until he is lawfully committed, discharged, or admitted to bail by order of the court.[56]

[51] Jones v. State, 26 Tex. App. 1; State v. Dennis, 2 Marv. (Del.) 433.

[52] Cantrill v. People, 3 Gil. (Ill.) 357; State v. Estis, 70 Mo. 427; State v. Hooker, 17 Vt. 658.

[53] State v. Leach, 7 Conn. 452; Housh v. People, 75 Ill. 491; State v. Beebe, 13 Kan. 589; People v. Ah-Teung, 92 Cal. 421; State v. Jones, 78 N. C. 420.

[54] Com. v. Tracey, 5 Metc. (Mass.) 552; State v. Garrett, 80 Iowa, 590.

[55] Wentworth v. People, 4 Scam. (Ill.) 555; State v. Freeman, 8 Iowa, 428.

[56] Com. v. Morihan, 4 Allen (Mass.), 585.

Escape.

§ 88. Definition. — Escape is departure of a prisoner from custody before he is discharged by due process of law.[57]

§ 89. Liability of Officer. — Should the officer, by his willingness or negligence, allow the prisoner to escape from his custody, he is liable.[58] It is not conclusive evidence of negligence against the officer that he did not handcuff his prisoner.[59]

If the escape is voluntary, and the prisoner was guilty of felony, the escape is a felony on the part of the officer.[60] If the escape is merely by the officer's negligence, it is only a misdemeanor in any case.

The only excuse that an officer can set up, when answering for the escape of a prisoner, is that it was by act of God, or the enemies of the country,[61] that is, the members of a nation at war with our country. But an officer is not criminally responsible for an escape by reason of the negligence of

---

[57] Bouvier's Law Dict. (Escape); Com. v. Farrell, 5 Allen (Mass.), 130; State v. Davis, 14 Nev. 446; Butler v. Washburn, 25 N. H. 251; Randall v. State, 53 N. J. L. 488; Ex parte Clifford, 29 Ind. 106; State v. Brown, 82 N. C. 585.

[58] State v. Ritchie, 107 N. C. 857; Garver v. Ter., 5 Okla. 342; Shattuck v. State, 51 Miss. 575.

[59] State v. Hunter, 94 N. C. 829.

[60] 2 Hawkins' Pl. C. c. 19, § 25.

[61] Fairchild v. Case, 24 Wend. (N. Y.) 383.

an assistant, if he used due care in selecting and appointing the assistant.[62]

If an officer makes an arrest, and has the prisoner admitted to bail in the same county, on an indorsed warrant issued in another county, he is guilty of a voluntary escape. In such case it is the officer's duty to retake the prisoner, and he may do so on the same warrant.[63]

And where a constable arrested the defendant on a warrant issued by a justice of the peace, and left him on his promise to follow him, and the accused was later arrested by a deputy sheriff, and taken to jail on a criminal process, so that the constable could not take him before the justice of the peace on the warrant, it was held that by the constable leaving his prisoner, after effecting the arrest, there was a voluntary escape, and the officer, being unable to retake him, was held liable for the escape.[64]

There can be no escape from custody where the arrest was made by a void warrant,[65] or where the act of taking into custody did not in itself amount to an arrest.

An officer may arrest with or without warrant[66]

---

[62] State *v.* Lewis, 113 N. C. 622.
[63] Clark *v.* Cleveland, 6 Hill (N. Y.), 344.
[64] Olmstead *v.* Raymond, 6 Johns. (N. Y.) 62.
[65] Housh *v.* People, 75 Ill. 487; Hitchcock *v.* Baker, 2 Allen (Mass.), 431.
[66] Com. *v.* Sheriff, 1 Grant (Pa.), 187; Floyd *v.* State, 79 Ala. 39; Clark *v.* Cleveland, 6 Hill (N. Y.), 344; State

one who has escaped from custody either before or after trial and commitment,[67] and it is immaterial whether the offence originally charged was a crime or misdemeanor, or whether the person escaping was guilty or innocent of the offence charged, because an unlawful departure from legal custody is always a criminal offence.[68] If an officer makes an illegal arrest, and then accepts a bribe from his prisoner to allow him to escape, he is guilty of bribery notwithstanding the arrest was illegal.[69]

v. Wamire, 16 Ind. 357; Hollon v. Hopkins, 21 Kan. 638. But see Doyle v. Russell, 30 Barb. (N. Y.) 300.

[67] McQueen v. State, 130 Ala. 136.

[68] Com. v. Miller, 2 Ashm. (Pa.) 68; Holland v. State, 60 Miss. 939; State v. Bates, 23 Iowa, 96.

[69] Mosely v. State, 25 Tex. App. 515.

CHAPTER V

ARREST WITH WARRANT

§ 90. Name of Arrested Party must appear in Warrant. — A warrant will not justify the arrest of one not named therein, by reason of the fact that the name used was supposed to be his.[1]

§ 91. Valid Warrant protects Officer. — If a warrant is lawful and regular on its face, disclosing no want of jurisdiction or other irregularity, and the magistrate issuing it has lawful authority to do so, the warrant is a complete protection to the officer who makes the arrest.[2] And a valid warrant protects an officer even though it be known that it was procured by fraud.[3]

§ 92. Invalid Warrant is no Protection. — If a warrant is not valid on its face, or if the whole subject-matter is without the jurisdiction of the

---

[1] West v. Cabell, 153 U. S. 78.

[2] Clark v. May, 2 Gray (Mass.), 410; Wright v. Keith, 24 Me. 158; Housh v. People, 75 Ill. 491; State v. James, 80 N. C. 370; Mangold v. Thorpe, 33 N. J. L. 134. See § 29, supra.

[3] Wilmarth v. Burt, 7 Metc. (Mass.) 257.

magistrate, the officer is really acting without any warrant at all, and thereby becomes a trespasser, if a private person under the same circumstances would be a trespasser. It is held by some authorities that the officer's life may be taken, if necessary, in resisting such unlawful arrest,[4] while other decisions hold that in case of an attempted illegal arrest by a known officer, it is not lawful to take life in resisting the arrest, and that if a person kills a known officer to prevent him making an illegal arrest, he is guilty of manslaughter at least,[5] and may be guilty of murder if the killing was prompted by personal malice against the officer.[6] If an officer kills in the act of serving void process, he is guilty of murder. And here it may be noted that throughout the law of arrest, the *necessity* of the case, when human life is to be taken, is of paramount importance, for nothing short of the sternest necessity will justify the act.

A party cannot reasonably apprehend any serious consequences to himself by submission to an illegal arrest by a known officer, beyond a temporary invasion of his right of personal liberty, and the law does not sanction the taking of life to repel every threatened trespass, or invasion of personal rights.[7]

---

[4] Com. *v.* Crotty, 10 Allen (Mass.), 403.
[5] State *v.* Cantieny, 34 Minn. 1.
[6] Rafferty *v.* People, 72 Ill. 37.
[7] Com. *v.* Drew, 4 Mass. 391; State *v.* Cantieny, supra cit.; Williams *v.* State, 44 Ala. 41.

§ 93. **When a Warrant is Void.** — A warrant is void if it has no seal,[8] when a seal is required by statute, or if it is not supported by sufficient oath or affirmation and that fact appear on its face,[9] or if it does not sufficiently describe the person to be arrested, so that from the description he may be identified;[10] as where a warrant is issued against "John Doe or Richard Roe, whose other or true name is to your complainant unknown," with no other description or means of identification, the warrant is absolutely void and may be resisted with all *necessary* force.[11]

§ 94. **Rights of Strangers to interfere.** — As a general rule, if the warrant be materially defective, or the officer exceeds his authority in executing it, any third person may lawfully interfere to prevent an arrest under it, doing no more than is actually necessary for that purpose.[12]

§ 95. **Liability of Officer's Assistant.** — If the officer is liable as a trespasser, especially in the service of civil process, the assistant of such officer may also be liable in trespass.[13]

[8] State *v.* Drake, 36 Me. 366. *Contra:* Millett *v.* Baker, 42 Barb. (N. Y.) 215. See § 50, supra.

[9] Grumon *v.* Raymond, 1 Conn. 40.

[10] Com. *v.* Crotty, 10 Allen (Mass.), 403.

[11] Com. *v.* Crotty, supra cit.

[12] Com. *v.* Crotty, supra cit.; Rex *v.* Osmer, 5 East (Eng. K. B.), 304.

[13] Darling *v.* Kelley, 113 Mass. 29.

§ 96. **Taking Prisoner before a Magistrate.** — The disposing of the prisoner becomes a very important matter after the consummation of a legal arrest, for if the disposition be not according to law, and as directed in the warrant,[14] the officer will render himself liable for the abuse of his process. The first duty after making the arrest is to bring the prisoner with all reasonable speed [15] before a magistrate for examination,[16] but if the prisoner is physically incapacitated to be so brought, or if from other circumstances an immediate hearing is impossible,[17] the officer may delay until the incapacity disappears, but no longer.

The warrant need not state the time when the party is to be brought before the magistrate for the examination,[18] but it being the duty of every

[14] 2 Hale's P. C. 119; Pratt *v.* Hill, 16 Barb. (N. Y.) 303.
[15] Green *v.* Kennedy, 46 Barb. (N. Y.) 16; Cary *v.* State, 76 Ala. 78; Habersham *v.* State, 56 Ga. 61.
[16] Brock *v.* Stimson, 108 Mass. 520; Ocean Steamship Co. *v.* Williams, 69 Ga. 251; Twilley *v.* Perkins, 77 Md. 252; Pastor *v.* Regan, 62 N. Y. St. 204; Judson *v.* Reardon, 16 Minn. 431; Cary *v.* State, 76 Ala. 78; Simmons *v.* Vandyke, 138 Ind. 380; State *v.* Freeman, 86 N. C. 683; Muscoe *v.* Com., 86 Va. 443; Missouri, etc. R. Co. *v.* Warner, 19 Tex. Civ. App. 463; Ashley *v.* Dundas, 5 Up. Can. Q. B. o. s. 749.
[17] Rohan *v.* Sawin, 5 Cush. (Mass.) 281; Wiggins *v.* Norton, 83 Ga. 148; State *v.* Freeman, 86 N. C. 683; Hutchinson *v.* Sangster, 4 Greene (Iowa), 340; Scircle *v.* Neeves, 47 Ind. 289.
[18] Mayhew *v.* Parker, 8 T. R. (Durnf. & E. Eng. K. B.) 110.

person who makes an arrest, whether he be an officer or a private party, to bring the prisoner before the proper magistrate without delay, a failure of the arresting party to do so promptly will make him guilty of false imprisonment.[19] Intoxication of the prisoner, for example, will excuse delay in this respect so long as the intoxication exists.[20] The duty to present the prisoner for examination is the same whether the arrest be with or without a warrant.

§ 97. **Officer's Right to release Prisoner.** — By the common law, an officer may make an arrest upon reasonable grounds of suspicion, and if his suspicions vanish, he may discharge the prisoner without bringing him before a magistrate.[21] But this provision of the common law does not authorize the officer to detain the prisoner for the purpose of verifying his suspicions.

§ 98. **Officer's Right to detain Prisoner.** — When an officer under a warrant from a county court, commanding him to arrest the respondent, and have him brought before that court forthwith,

---

[19] Porter v. Swindle, 3 S. E. Rep. (Ga.) 94; Burke v. Bell, 36 Me. 317.

[20] Arneson v. Thorstad, 33 N. W. Rep. (Iowa), 607; Wiltse v. Holt, 95 Ind. 469; Scircle v. Neeves, 47 Ind. 289; State v. Freeman, 86 N. C. 683; Hutchinson v. Sangster, 4 Greene (Iowa), 340.

[21] Burke v. Bell, supra cit.

arrests the respondent, brings him to the place of holding such court, but finds the court not in session, he may detain the respondent a reasonable time until he can ascertain whether it is possible to deliver him into court, and may lodge him in jail in the mean time for safe-keeping.[22]

§ 99. **Impossibility as a Defence.** — It sometimes happens that it becomes impossible for an officer to perform a duty which the law has commanded him to do, but the impossibility is a good defence to an indictment for not performing the duty.[23]

If, for example, an officer has been commanded to deliver a prisoner to a certain official, or to have him at a certain place, and the official or the place has ceased to exist, the officer is excused from the performance of the command of the law, and would be justified in confining his prisoner in a suitable place until further order could be procured from the court for the disposition of the prisoner.

§ 100. **The Place of Confinement.** — Even a freight car is not, as a matter of law, an unsuitable place for confining a prisoner.[24] But it might be, as a matter of fact for a jury to consider, as, for example, if the freight car should expose the prisoner to the inclemency of the weather, or otherwise endanger his health. So where an officer arrested

---

[22] Kent v. Miles, 65 Vt. 582.
[23] Tate v. State, 5 Blackf. (Ind.) 73.
[24] Arneson v. Thorstad, 33 N. W. Rep. (Iowa), 607.

one upon a charge of drunkenness, and confined him in the city guard-house, where during the night the prisoner died, the jury finding that his death was "accelerated by the noxious air of the guard-house," the city was held liable for thus improperly confining the prisoner.[25]

An officer being responsible for the safety of his prisoner, the place of confinement is left largely to his discretion. And it was held that a United States marshal was justified in confining his prisoner in the State Penitentiary instead of the county jail, when, in his opinion, the safety and security of the prisoner required it.[26]

§ 101. **Exercise of Officer's own Judgment.** — The question of what constitutes reasonable necessity very frequently arises in matters pertaining to the law of arrest. And it may be said that whenever an officer is called upon to exercise his own judgment, in any matter, the law not instructing him as to the course which he shall pursue, he is not liable if he does that, which, considering all the circumstances of the case, any other man of fair average intelligence would do under similar circumstances. That is, he is not required to exercise the highest grade of judgment, but he must not fall below that which is expected from the man of a fair average intellect.

And any act or omission of an officer which arises

---

[25] Lewis *v.* City of Raleigh, 77 N. C. 229.
[26] Clinton *v.* Nelson, 2 Utah, 284.

from the necessity of the case, will justify the officer in acting or not acting only so long as the necessity exists.[27]

§ 102. **Prisoner may waive Right to be taken before a Magistrate.** — When the statute provides that the person arrested be brought before a magistrate, the officer is liable for false arrest if he discharges the prisoner without bringing him before a magistrate, unless there is an express waiver by the prisoner of his right to be taken before a magistrate.[28]

As where an officer arrested the accused for intoxication, between one and two o'clock in the morning, on a Sunday, and detained him until between seven and eight o'clock in the afternoon of the next day, when it was found that the trial justice was detained out of town by reason of an unusual freshet which had rendered travelling unsafe. These facts were communicated to the accused, and upon his own request he was released from custody. *Held*, that an action for false imprisonment did not lie.[29]

When, however, the arrest is by warrant, the duty of the officer to take the prisoner before a magistrate is an absolute duty; therefore the prisoner may not then waive his right to be taken

---

[27] Tubbs *v.* Tukey, 3 Cush. (Mass.) 438.

[28] Brock *v.* Stimson, 108 Mass. 520; Phillips *v.* Fadden, 125 Mass. 198; Caffrey *v.* Drugan, 144 Mass. 294.

[29] Caffrey *v.* Drugan, supra cit.

before the magistrate, and nothing except impossibility will excuse the officer from obeying the command of the law.

CIVIL ARREST.[30]

§ 103. **Constitutional Prohibitions. — Fraud.** — Imprisonment for debt arising out of contract is generally prohibited by constitutional provisions;[31] but these provisions do not apply where fraud is a factor in the charge[32] And the fraud charged must relate to procuring the contract to be made, or in attempting to evade performance.[33]

Constitutional or statutory abolishments of imprisonment for debt do not apply to tort actions,[34] although the right to arrest in tort actions is extensively regulated by the statutes of the several States. Nor do they apply to arrest for the nonpayment of taxes.[35]

§ 104. **Statutes must be Strictly followed.** — A statute authorizing an arrest on civil process must be so strictly construed that process will only

---

[30] Refer to index for other matters pertaining to this subject.

[31] Act of Congress, Feb. 28, 1839.

[32] Appleton v. Hopkins, 5 Gray (Mass.), 530.

[33] In re Tyson, 32 Mich. 262.

[34] McDuffie v. Beddoe, 7 Hill (N. Y.), 578; U. S. v. Banister, 70 Fed. Rep. (U. S.) 44; Sedgebeer v. Moore, Brightley (Pa.), 197.

[35] Appleton v. Hopkins, supra cit.

issue in cases that are clearly within the statute,[36] and all the proceedings in the arrest must strictly follow the statutory provisions.

§ 105. **Debtor about to leave State.** — Where the statute provides for the arrest of a debtor who is about to leave the State with intent to avoid the payment of his debts, he is not subject to such arrest if he leaves for a temporary absence only,[37] or if he leaves sufficient property within the State for the payment of the particular debt for which he is arrested, although he does not leave sufficient property for the payment of all his debts,[38] or if he leaves the State for the *bona fide* purpose of seeking employment elsewhere, or improving his condition.[39]

§ 106. **Must be a Fraudulent Intent.** — To justify the arrest, an intent to defraud must be proved.[40] A fraudulent intent also must be proved where an arrest is under a statute authorizing an arrest for the fraudulent concealment of property from a creditor. Therefore, one who wears his watch and carries his money with him in his usual manner is

---

[36] Merritt *v.* Openheim, 9 La. Ann. 54; Hathaway *v.* Johnson, 55 N. Y. 93.

[37] Myall *v.* Wright, 2 Bush (Ky.), 130.

[38] Carraby *v.* Davis, 6 Mart. N. S. (La.) 163.

[39] Stevenson *v.* Smith, 28 N. H. 12.

[40] Tramblay *v.* Graham, 7 Montreal Super. Ct. 374; Devries *v.* Summit, 86 N. C. 126; Hudson's Case, 2 Mart. (La.) 172.

not guilty of the fraudulent intent which is essential to the maintenance of the action.[41]

§ 107. **Affidavit required by Statute.** — The usual statutory provisions relating to the application for the writ or warrant for a civil arrest require that an affidavit be filed setting forth the facts constituting the cause for arrest.

This affidavit must state that the affiant believes and has reason to believe that the defendant has property not exempt from execution which he does not intend to apply to plaintiff's claim.[42]

If the arrest is to be made because the defendant is about to leave the State, the affidavit must not only state that the defendant is about to leave the State, but must also aver that the affiant believes that the debtor is leaving with intent to defraud his creditors, after which probable cause for entertaining the belief should be shown by setting forth the facts upon which the belief is based.[43]

§ 108. **Effect of Altering Writ.** — If the writ is altered before it is served, a new affidavit is necessary or the arrest will be illegal.[44]

§ 109. **No Arrest after Attachment.** — An arrest made after an attachment of property in the same action is altogether void.[45]

[41] Clement *v.* Dudley, 42 N. H. 367.
[42] Stone *v.* Carter, 13 Gray (Mass.), 575.
[43] Wilson *v.* Barnhill, 64 N. C. 121.
[44] Amadon *v.* Mann, 3 Gray (Mass.), 467.
[45] Almy *v.* Wolcott, 13 Mass. 76.

§ 110. **Officer's Liability for Escape.** — An officer has authority to call for assistance in making an arrest on mesne process, but he is not obliged to do so. And he is not liable for an escape that might have been prevented by his calling for aid, if the party arrested by him rescues himself or is rescued by others.[46]

§ 111. **Insolvency Proceedings.** — Where a defendant has been legally arrested in a civil action, and while in custody files his voluntary petition in insolvency, he is not thereby entitled to be released from arrest.[47]

---

[46] Whitehead *v.* Keyes, 3 Allen (Mass.), 500; Sutton *v.* Allison, 2 Jones (N. C.), 341.

[47] Hussey *v.* Danforth, 77 Me. 17.

CHAPTER VI

ARREST WITHOUT A WARRANT

§ 112. By Private Person in Case of Felony. — A private person may arrest without a warrant one whom he sees committing a felony, or when a felony has been actually committed, and he has reasonable grounds within his own knowledge — that is, not merely from the hearsay evidence of the statements of third persons — for believing that the person whom he places under arrest is the felon.[1] But he has no right to make an arrest without a warrant when a felony has not in fact been committed, no matter how well founded may have been his belief that a felony had been committed. In other words, an arrest for felony by a private person without a warrant is lawful only when a felony has actually been committed, and he can justify his act of arrest by proof of the commission of the felony.[2]

---

[1] Holley v. Mix, 3 Wend. (N. Y.) 351; Ashley's Case, 12 Coke (Eng. K. B.), 90; Dodds v. Board, 43 Ill. 95; State v. Mowry, 37 Kan. 369; Kennedy v. State, 107 Ind. 144; Brooks v. Com., 61 Pa. St. 352; Long v. State, 12 Ga. 293; Wright v. Com., 85 Ky. 123.

[2] " Even when there is only probable cause of suspicion, a private person may, without warrant, *at his peril*, make an arrest. I say at his peril, for nothing short of proving the

If a felony has actually been committed, a private person is justified in arresting one whom he has good reason to believe to be guilty of it, even though the person arrested should afterward be proven to be innocent.[3]

§ 113. **Assisting a Private Person.** — A private person who has no reasonable grounds within his own knowledge to believe that a felony has been committed, has no right to assist another private person in making an arrest, who is acting without a warrant upon reasonable suspicion which would justify him in making the arrest.[4] But if a private person knows that the one whom he seeks to arrest

---

felony will justify the arrest," TILGHMAN, C. J., in Wakely v. Hart, 6 Binn. (Pa.) 316; Geary v. Stephenson, 169 Mass. 23; Carr v. State, 43 Ark. 99; Teagarden v. Graham, 31 Ind. 422; Davis v. U. S., 16 App. Cas. (D. C.) 442; Croom v. State, 85 Ga. 718; Kindred v. Stitt, 51 Ill. 101; Siegel v. Connor, 70 Ill. App. 116; Cryer v. State, 71 Miss. 467; Simmerman v. State, 16 Neb. 615; Reuck v. McGregor, 32 N. J. 70; Farnam v. Feeley, 56 N. Y. 451; People v. Hochstim, 36 Misc. Rep. (N. Y.) 562; State v. Morgan, 22 Utah, 162; McCarthy v. De Armitt, 99 Pa. St. 63; Burch v. Franklin, 7 Ohio N. P. 155; Neal v. Joyner, 89 N. C. 287; U. S. v. Boyd, 45 Fed. Rep. (U. S.) 851. "Any one may arrest a thief without a warrant." Wrexford v. Smith, 2 Root (Conn.), 171.

[3] Holley v. Mix, supra cit.; Habersham v. State, 56 Ga. 61; Wilson v. State, 11 Lea (Tenn.), 310; Brockway v. Crawford, 48 N. C. 433; Farnam v. Feeley, 56 N. Y. 451; McKenzie v. Gibson, 8 Up. Can. Q. B. 100.

[4] Salisbury v. Com., 79 Ky. 425.

is a felon, he may command the assistance of a bystander.[5]

§ 114. **Hue and Cry.** — Under a "hue and cry," however, a private person may make an arrest, even though it should subsequently be shown that no felony had been committed.

What is a Felony?

§ 115. **Definition.** — In English common law a felony comprised the commission of any species of crime which occasioned the total forfeiture of land and goods.[6]

But this definition does not apply in the United States, because the Constitution of the United States, Article I, Section 12, provides that "no conviction shall work corruption of blood, *or forfeiture of estate.*" Therefore an accurate definition of a felony can be found only in the statutes of the particular State wherein the offence is committed. The courts will not construe an offence to be a felony unless such construction is made necessary by the express words of the statute, or by necessary implication,[7] for the statutes are to be construed so as not to multiply felonies.[8]

[5] 2 Hale's P. C. 76.

[6] Ex parte Wilson, 114 U. S. 417, 423, citing 4 Blackstone's Commentaries, 94, 95, 310; Com. v. Carey, 12 Cush. (Mass.) 246; B. & W. R. Co. v. Dana, 1 Gray (Mass.), 83.

[7] Wilson v. State, 1 Wis. 163.

[8] Com. v. Carey, 12 Cush. (Mass.) 246; Com. v. Carroll, 8 Mass. 490; Wilson v. State, supra cit.

Perhaps a fair statutory definition of a felony in the United States is as follows: "A crime which is punishable by death or imprisonment in the State prison is a felony. All other crimes are misdemeanors." [9]

§ 116. **By Private Person in Case of Misdemeanor.** — In misdemeanors, the right of a private person to arrest without a warrant is limited to cases of breach of the peace committed in the presence of the arresting party,[10] or to prevent the continuation of a breach of the peace which has temporarily stopped, but which he has good and reasonable ground to believe will continue but for the arrest.[11] Without a warrant he cannot make an arrest to prevent the commission of an affray or breach of the peace which has not yet begun, but which is simply apprehensive, nor can he arrest without a warrant one who has committed a breach of the peace after the act had been completed.[12]

---

[9] Revised Laws of Mass. c. 215, § 1.

[10] People v. Morehouse, 6 N. Y. Suppl. 763; Phillips v. Trull, 11 Johns. (N. Y.) 486; Knot v. Gay, 1 Root (Conn.), 66; Price v. Seeley, 10 Cl. & F. (Eng. H. L.) 28; Forrester v. Clarke, 3 Up. Can. Q. B. 151; State v. Campbell, 107 N. C. 948; Com. v. McNall, 1 Woodw. (Pa.) 423; Barclay v. U. S., 11 Okla. 503.

[11] Price v. Seeley, supra cit.; Ingle v. Bell, 1 M. & W. (Eng. Exch.) 516.

[12] Shanley v. Wells, 71 Ill. 78.

What is a Breach of the Peace?

§ 117. Definition. — The public peace is that sense of security which every person feels, and which is necessary to his comfort, and for which government is instituted; and a breach of the public peace is the invasion of the security and protection which the law affords every citizen.[13]

A breach of the peace is a violation of public order, the offence of disturbing the public peace. An act of public indecorum is also a breach of the peace.[14]

§ 118. Inciting Others to break the Peace. — Anything which tends to provoke or excite others to break the peace is in itself a breach of the peace.[15] So where a striker meets a non-union workman on the street, and calls him "a damned scab," the language, tending to provoke a conflict, is a breach of the peace.[16] So is calling one "sheep thief," and following him, bleating like a sheep.[17] And to call a man a "damn fool" and a "bastard" is a breach of the peace.[18]

---

[13] State v. Archibald, 59 Vt. 548.
[14] Bouvier's Law Dict. (Breach of Peace); Galvin v. State, 46 Tenn. 283.
[15] 4 Bl. Com. 150.
[16] Com. v. Redshaw, 12 Pa. Co. Ct. 91; Com. v. Silvers, 11 Pa. Co. Ct. 481.
[17] State v. Warner, 34 Conn. 276.
[18] Topeka v. Heitman, 47 Kan. 739.

§ 119. **No Defence that Words are True.** — The essence of the offence of breaking the peace being the disturbance of the public tranquillity, it is no defence that opprobrious words, tending to provoke violence, are true.[19]

§ 120. **Doing Lawful Act in a Turbulent Manner.** — Where one attempts to abate a public nuisance, in such a manner as to invite resistance, he is guilty of a breach of the peace. As where the defendant, armed with a pitchfork, hoe, and pistol, proceeds to remove an obstruction in the highway, knowing that the one who placed the obstruction there is guarding it, is guilty of a breach of the peace.[20] Breaking the locks of doors in such a manner as to provoke a breach of the peace, is a breach of the peace in itself.[21]

§ 121. **Violent Language.** — Where the plaintiff, in a loud and boisterous manner, called the defendant, a police officer, a " God-damned son of a bitch," and other names, and threatened to kill the officer if he attempted to arrest him, the plaintiff was guilty of a breach of the peace.[22]

If a man stops before the door of a dwelling-

---

[19] Dyer *v.* State, 99 Ga. 20.
[20] State *v.* White, 18 R. I. 473; State *v.* Flanagan, 67 Ind. 140; Day *v.* Day, 4 Md. 262.
[21] Taafe *v.* Kyne, 9 Mo. App. 15.
[22] Davis *v.* Burgess, 54 Mich. 514.

house or shop and uses violent language toward the inmates, and thereby attracts a crowd, and will not desist when requested, he is guilty of a breach of the peace.[23] So also if he uses loud and violent language in his own dwelling-house, addressed to inmates thereof, if the disturbance is such as to attract a gathering of persons outside of his house, this is a breach of the peace.[24] And with much stronger reason would this amount to a breach of the peace if done in a public place.[25]

§ 122. **Discharging Firearms.** — The wanton discharge of a firearm in a public street of a city is a breach of the peace.[26] And where the defendant went to the house of the complaining witness, armed with a gun, during the absence of the male members of the family, and from the porch thereof shot and killed two of his dogs, which were lying in the yard, and thereby terrified the females in the house, such action constitutes a breach of the peace for which an indictment will lie.[27]

§ 123. **Disturbing Public Worship.** — The disturbance of public worship is an act tending to destroy

---

[23] Cohen v. Huskisson, 2 M. & W. (Eng. Exch.) 482. But see Ware v. Leveridge, 75 Mich. 488. Compare State v. Schuermann, 52 Mo. 165.

[24] Com. v. Foley, 99 Mass. 497.

[25] McCandless v. State, 2 S. W. Rep. (Tex.) 811.

[26] People v. Bartz, 53 Mich. 493.

[27] Henderson v. Com., 8 Gratt. (Va.) 708.

the public morals, and amounts to a breach of the peace.[28]

§ 124. PROSTITUTES. — A prostitute who, on the street, or while sitting at the window of her room, solicits men from the streets for immoral purposes, is guilty of the offence.[29] But an officer may not arrest one reputed a common prostitute who has committed no offence in his presence.[30]

§ 125. MUST BE A PUBLIC DISTURBANCE. — An act cannot constitute a breach of the peace unless it disturbs the public, that is to say, an indefinite number of persons. Therefore charging one with being a prostitute and keeping a house of ill fame, if the statement does not in itself tend to disturb others, is not a breach of the peace.[31]

§ 126. PUBLIC SHOUTING. — Shouting in the streets of a village between nine and ten o'clock in the evening, so loudly as to be heard one hundred and fifty feet distant, is a breach of the peace.[32] But

[28] U. S. *v.* Brooks, 4 Cranch C. C. (U. S) 427.
But a Sunday-school is not a place of religious " worship." Hubbard *v.* State, 32 Tex. Cr. 391. *Contra:* State *v.* Stuth, 11 Wash. 423.

[29] Harft *v.* McDonald, 1 City Ct. Rep. (N. Y. City) 181; People *v.* Pratt, 22 Hun (N. Y.), 300.

[30] In re Sarah Way, 41 Mich. 299; Pinkerton *v.* Verberg, 78 Mich. 573. *Contra:* Shafer *v.* Mumma, 17 Md. 331.

[31] State *v.* Schlottman, 52 Mo. 164.

[32] People *v.* Johnson, 86 Mich. 175. But see Mundini *v.* State, 37 Tex. Cr. 5; Hardy *v.* Murphy, 1 Esp. (Eng. N. P.) 294.

when the officer heard it from another street, and did not see the offender, the offence was not committed in his presence, and an arrest without a warrant would not be justifiable, because the officer had no direct knowledge that it was he who had committed the offence.[33] Driving a carriage through the streets of a populous city in such a manner as to endanger the safety of the inhabitants, was at common law an indictable offence, and is a breach of the peace.[34]

§ 127. **Swearing.—Drunkenness.**—Profane swearing is a breach of the peace,[35] and so is public and disorderly drunkenness.[36]

§ 128. **Use of Force, by Private Person.**—A private person attempting to make an arrest in case of a felony may, in those cases where a private person can lawfully arrest, use all force necessary to accomplish the arrest, even to the taking of life. So also may he kill to prevent the commission of a felony, when it cannot be otherwise prevented.

But a private person has no right to arrest one

---

[33] People v. Johnson, 86 Mich. 175. But see People v. Bartz, 53 Mich. 493.

[34] U. S. v. Hart, Pet. C. C. (U. S.) 390.

[35] Holcomb v. Cornish, 8 Conn. 375; Com. v. Linn, 158 Pa. St. 22; State v. Chrisp, 85 N. C. 528.

[36] State v. Lafferty, 5 Harr. (Del.) 491; Bryan v. Bates, 15 Ill. 87; State v. Freeman, 86 N. C. 683. But see Com. v. O'Connor, 7 Allen (Mass.), 583, holding it no crime at common law.

for whom he knows that a warrant has been issued for an assault with intent to commit murder, unless at the time he is assisting the officer who has the warrant.[27]

§ 129. **Arrest by Officer without a Warrant.** — An officer may arrest without a warrant, whenever a private person may do so; and his authority extends beyond that of a private person in that he may arrest without a warrant one whom he has reasonable ground [38] to suspect has committed a felony, whether he acts upon his own knowledge, or by facts communicated by others;[39] and if reasonable grounds exist for the suspicion, he is protected, although no crime of any sort has been committed.[40]

[27] Kirbie v. State, 5 Tex. App. 60.

[38] Davis v. U. S., 16 App. Cas. (D. C.) 442; Kirk v. Garrett, 84 Md. 383; Williams v. State, 44 Ala. 41; Chandler v. Rutherford, 101 Fed. Rep. (U. S.) 774; Ex parte Morrill, 13 Sawy. (U. S.) 322; Tooley's Case, 2 Ld. Raymond (Eng. K. B.) 1296; Filer v. Smith, 96 Mich. 347; People v. Burt, 51 Mich. 199; Fulton v. Staats, 41 N. Y. 498; Hedges v Chapman, 2 Bing. (Eng. C. P.) 523; Hamilton v. Calder, 23 N. Bruns. 373.

[39] Holley v. Mix, 3 Wend. (N. Y.) 350; Filer v. Smith, 96 Mich. 347; Chandler v. Rutherford, 101 Fed. Rep. (U. S) 774; Williams v. State, 44 Ala. 41.

[40] Danovan v. Jones, 36 N. H. 246; Com. v. Cheney, 141 Mass. 102; Holley v. Mix, 3 Wend. (N. Y.) 351; State v. Symes, 20 Wash. 484; Muscoe v. Com., 86 Va. 443; State v. Taylor, 70 Vt. 1; Wade v. Chaffee, 8 R. I. 224; Neal v. Joyner, 89 N. C. 287; State v. Grant, 76 Mo. 236; Kirk

§ 130. **Suspicion must be well Founded.** — But an officer has no right to arrest on suspicion that is not well founded, as in case of a mere suspicion not supported by facts, circumstances, or credible information.[41] Thus the information given by an accomplice is not sufficient to justify an arrest.[42] And neither an officer nor a private person in making an arrest upon suspicion without a warrant has a right to kill the supposed felon, either to effect the arrest or prevent an escape, except in self-defence.[43]

§ 131. **Arrest for Violation of a City Ordinance.** — An officer, may also arrest, without a warrant, one who in his presence commits a breach of the peace;[44] and by authority of statute, city charter, or

v. Garrett, 84 Md. 383; Wright v. Com., 85 Ky. 123; Bright v. Patton, 5 Mackey (D. C.), 534; People v. Pool, 27 Cal. 572; Lewis v. State, 3 Head (Tenn.), 127; State v. West, 3 Ohio St. 509; Burns v. Erben, 40 N. Y. 463; People v. Hochstim, 36 Misc. Rep. (N. Y.) 562; McCarthy v. De Armitt, 99 Pa. St. 63; Diers v. Mallow, 46 Neb. 121; Doering v. State, 49 Ind. 56; Scott v. Eldridge, 154 Mass. 25; Williams v. State, 44 Ala. 41; Carr v. State, 43 Ark. 99; Filer v. Smith, 96 Mich. 347; Hadley v. Perks, L. R. 1 Q. B. 444. But see Marsh v. Smith, 49 Ill. 396; Warner v. Grace, 14 Minn. 487; Cryer v. State, 71 Miss. 467.

[41] People v. Burt, 51 Mich. 199; Williams v. State, 44 Ala. 41.

[42] Wills v. Jordan, 20 R. I. 630.

[43] Brooks v. Com., 61 Pa. St. 352; Conraddy v. People, 5 Park. Cr. (N. Y.), 234. *Contra:* Shanley v. Wells, 71 Ill. 78.

[44] Com. v. Tobin, 108 Mass. 426; Tracy v. Williams, 4 Conn. 107; Douglass v. Barber, 18 R. I. 459; In re Powers,

ordinance,[45] he may arrest without a warrant, one who, within his jurisdiction, commits a misdemeanor other than a breach of the peace, as, for example, one who is violating a city ordinance, without breaking the peace,[46] although by the common law he would have no authority to do so.[47]

There is a tendency on part of the courts to look with disfavor upon legislative enactments that authorize arrests without warrants for misdemeanors not amounting to breaches of the peace,[48] as interfering with the constitutional liberties of the subject.[49]

§ 132. **Special Authority may justify Officer in arresting for Misdemeanor not committed in his Presence.** — When specially authorized, — as by the city charter of Chicago, — an officer may arrest either with or without warrant, for a breach of the peace or threat to break the peace, even though the breach

---

25 Vt. 261; State v. Russell, 1 Houst. Cr. (Del.) 122; Fleetwood v. Com., 80 Ky. 2; Boutte v. Emmer, 43 La. 980; State v. Guy, 46 La. 1441; Hayes v. Mitchell, 80 Ala. 183; Veneman v. Jones, 118 Ind. 41; Beville v. State, 16 Tex. App. 70.

[45] Main v. McCarty, 15 Ill. 441; Roderick v. Whitson, 51 Hun (N. Y.), 620; White v. Kent, 11 Ohio St. 550.

[46] Union Depot, etc. Co. v. Smith, 16 Col. 361.

[47] Tillman v. Beard, 121 Mich. 475; Judson v. Reardon, 16 Minn. 431.

[48] People v. Haug, 37 N. W. Rep. (Mich.) 21.

[49] Jamison v. Gaernett, 10 Bush (Ky.), 221. *Contra:* Butolph v. Blust, 41 How. Pr. (N. Y.) 481.

or threat was not committed in the presence of the arresting officer.[50] But a mere threat to break the peace will not justify an arrest without a warrant, unless the threat is acccmpanied by an open act in the attempted execution thereof.[51]

§ 133. **Presence is presumed.** — When an officer makes an arrest for a breach of the peace, there is a *prima facie* presumption that he had a warrant, or that the offence was committed in his presence.[52]

§ 134. **What is meant by ' Presence."** — By presence of the officer is meant that he must actually see the offence committed; being near enough to see is not sufficient,[53] unless he hears it and immediately proceeds to the scene.[54] And if within his vision, it is immaterial that it was at a distance.[55]

§ 135. **Arrest Outside of Officer's Jurisdiction.** — An officer has no authority to make an arrest outside of his jurisdiction, even with a warrant, except in those cases in which a private person may act without a warrant. Then an officer may make the arrest, not by virtue of his office, for that is limited

[50] Main *v.* McCarty, 15 Ill. 441.
[51] Quinn *v.* Heisel, 40 Mich. 576.
[52] Davis *v.* Pac. Telephone, etc. Co., 127 Cal. 312.
[53] Russell *v.* State, 37 Tex. Cr. 314.
[54] Ramsey *v.* State, 92 Ga. 53; State *v.* McAfee, 107 N. C. 812; Dilger *v.* Com., 88 Ky. 550; State *v.* Williams, 36 S. C. 493; Brooks *v.* State, 114 Ga. 6; Hawkins *v.* Lutton, 95 Wis. 492.
[55] People *v.* Bartz, 53 Mich. 493.

by his jurisdiction, but by that right which the law places upon him as a citizen owing a duty to the State.[56]

§ 136. **Effect of Submission to Illegal Arrest.** — A person arrested by an officer outside of his jurisdiction who fails to object at the time of the arrest, and voluntarily accompanies the officer, thereby waives the illegality of the arrest, and cannot subsequently object to it as for that reason illegal.[57]

§ 137. **Arrest for Fraud.** — At the request of a keeper of a restaurant, a police officer has no right to arrest without a warrant, one who, in taking a meal at a restaurant, fraudulently substitutes the check given him for one of less amount, which latter he pays,[58] because it was not a criminal act, nor did it tend *immediately* to create a breach of the peace.

§ 138. **Entering Unfastened Door to arrest for Breach of the Peace.** — A constable, or other peace officer, has a right, by virtue of his office, without a warrant, to enter through an unfastened door, a house in which there is a noise amounting to a disturbance of the peace, and arrest any one disturbing the peace there in his presence.[59]

[56] 2 Hale's P. C. 115; Ressler v. Peats, 86 Ill. 275.
[57] In re Popejoy, 26 Col. 32.
[58] Boyleston v. Kerr, 2 Daly (N. Y.), 220.
[59] Com. v. Tobin, 103 Mass. 426; Ford v. Breen, 173 Mass. 52.

§ 139. **Entering Fastened Door to arrest for Breach of the Peace.** — After announcing his authority, an officer may, upon demanding and being refused admittance, break open a fastened door even at night, for the purpose of suppressing or preventing a breach of the peace and making an arrest therefor.[60] But a private person may not,[61] except to prevent a felony.[62]

§ 140. **Entering to arrest for Peaceable Drunkenness.** — When the statute authorizes an arrest for "drunkenness by the voluntary use of intoxicating liquor," the officer may take the guilty party from her own room in her own dwelling-house, where she is making no disturbance, and is not exposed to public view, but is lying in a drunken stupor; because the *place* where the offence is committed is not an element to be considered in determining whether the accused person is guilty under the law.[63] And the legality or illegality of the arrest does not in any way affect the offence with which she is charged,[64] although if entrance to her house for the purpose of making the arrest was obtained

---

[60] McLennon v. Richardson, 15 Gray (Mass.), 74; State v. Lafferty, 5 Harr. (Del.) 491; State v. Stouderman, 6 La. Ann. 286; McCullough v. Com., 67 Pa. St. 30.; Rex v. Smith, 6 C. & P. (Eng. N. P.) 136.

[61] Rockwell v. Murray, 6 Up. Can. Q. B. 412.

[62] Handcock v. Baker, 2 B. & P. (Eng. C. P.) 260.

[63] Com. v. Conlin, 184 Mass. 195.

[64] Ibid.

illegally, she would have an action against the arresting party for the trespass.

§ 141. **Arrest without Warrant for Breach of the Peace must be Immediate.** — Though at common law an officer might without warrant arrest for a breach of the peace committed in his view, the arrest must have been made at the time of, or within a reasonable time after, the commission of the offence,[65] — that is, the officer must immediately set about the arrest, and follow up the effort until the arrest is made. There must be a continued pursuit and no cessation of acts tending toward the arrest from the time of the commission of the offence until the apprehension of the offender.[66] Any delay for purposes foreign to the arrest will make the officer a trespasser.

Where the officer saw the defendant committing a misdemeanor in the street, and went for another officer, returning in half an hour, when he arrested the defendant, he was held to be justified.[67] But a delay of two hours has been held unjustifiable.[68]

§ 142. **Stale Offence Less than Felony requires a Warrant.** — In all cases not felonies, or likely to result in one, where the offence is not committed

[65] Wahl v. Walton, 30 Minn. 506.
[66] Ibid.
[67] Butolph v. Blust, 5 Lans. (N. Y.) 84.
[68] Reg. v. Walker, 6 Cox C. C. (Eng.) 371 ; see also Joyce v. Parkhurst, 150 Mass. 243; Com. v. Ruggles, 6 Allen (Mass.), 588.

in the officer's view, or the act done or threat made is not fresh, a constable or policeman has no authority to make an arrest without a warrant.[69] So where an officer arrests a person, under a city ordinance, as a vagrant, not having a visible means of support, the offence, if there was one, being a misdemeanor not committed in his presence, he is liable in trespass.[70]

§ 143. **Arrest of Person Rightfully standing near Sidewalk.** — Except on charge of felony an officer has no right to arrest without a warrant, one whom he finds peaceably standing in front of his place of residence, between the sidewalk and building, who is not creating a disturbance.[71]

§ 144. **Pursuit of Felon.** — In case of a dangerous wounding, whereby a felony is likely to ensue, an officer may, upon probable suspicion, without a warrant, arrest the party causing the wound, and for that purpose is authorized to break doors, or even kill the felon, if he cannot otherwise be taken.[72]

§ 145. **Duty of Private Person to arrest a Felon.** — Any private person, and with much stronger reason any officer, that is present when any felony is committed is bound by the law to arrest the felon, on pain of fine and imprisonment if he escapes

[69] Shanley *v.* Wells, 71 Ill. 78.
[70] Ibid.
[71] Com. *v.* Ridgeway, 2 Pa. Dist. 59.
[72] 2 Hale's P. C. 88; Shanley *v.* Wells, supra cit.; 4 Bl. Com. 292.

through the negligence of the standers-by.[73] And they may justify breaking open the doors upon following such felon; and if they kill him, provided he cannot otherwise be taken, it is justifiable;[74] though if they are killed in endeavoring to make such arrest, it is murder.[75]

§ 146. **Arrest under a General Authority.** — A police officer has the right to arrest, without a warrant, under the general power conferred upon the police force to prevent crime and arrest offenders, a person found violating the sanitary ordinances of a city.[76]

Under a statute which authorizes marshals to "arrest and detain any person found violating any law," a marshal of a municipal corporation is authorized to arrest without warrant a person found carrying concealed weapons contrary to law, although he has no previous personal knowledge of the fact, if he acts *bona fide*, and upon such information as induces an honest belief that the person arrested is in the act of violating the law.[77]

[73] 2 Hawkin's P. C. 74; 4 Bl. Com. 293; Long *v.* State, 12 Ga. 293.

[74] 4 Bl. Com. 292; Foster (Eng.), 271; U. S. *v.* Clark, 31 Fed. Rep. (U. S.) 710; Thomas *v.* Kinkead, 55 Ark. 502; Conraddy *v.* People, 5 Park. Cr. (N. Y.) 234; Reneau *v.* State, 2 Lea (Tenn.), 720; Brown *v.* Weaver, 76 Miss. 7; Head *v.* Martin, 85 Ky. 480; State *v.* Sigman, 106 N. C. 728.

[75] 2 Hale's P. C. 77.

[76] Mitchell *v.* Lemon, 34 Md. 176.

[77] Ballard *v.* State, 43 Ohio St. 340.

§ 147. **Arrest of Deserters from United States Army.** — The rule of the common law, that an officer or private person may arrest a felon without a warrant, has never been extended to the case of an offender against the military law, punishable exclusively by court-martial. Therefore an officer or a private person, without order or direction of a military officer, has no right to arrest or detain a deserter from the army of the United States.[78] Nor can a military officer lawfully break into a dwelling-house for the purpose of capturing a deserter.[79]

§ 148. **Arrest by a Bail.** — A bail may arrest his principal at any time and anywhere, even in another State, using no violence unless there is resistance. And he may delegate the power to another in writing to do it for him. But the party to whom the power is delegated cannot delegate the power to another, although he may call in others to assist him in making the arrest.[80]

A bail, or one authorized by him, after due notice, demand of admittance, and refusal, may forcibly enter a dwelling-house to effect the arrest of the principal.[81]

---

[78] Kurtz v. Moffitt, 115 U. S. 487.

[79] Clay v. U. S., Dev. Ct. Cl. (U. S.) 25.

[80] State v. Mahon, 3 Harr. (Del.) 568; Taylor v. Taintor, 16 Wall. (U. S.) 366; In re Von Der Ahe, 85 Fed. Rep. (U. S.) 959.

[81] Read v. Case, 4 Conn. 166.

§ 149. **Arrest to prevent Crime.** — With respect to interference and arrests in order to prevent the commission of a crime, any person may lay hold of a lunatic about to commit any mischief which, if committed by a sane person, would constitute a criminal offence,[82] or any other person whom he shall see on the point of committing a treason or felony, or doing any act which will manifestly endanger the life or person of another, and may detain him until it may be reasonably presumed that he has changed his purpose. Thus, any one may justify breaking and entering a party's house and imprisoning him, to prevent him from murdering his wife, who cries out for assistance.[83]

Where one interferes to prevent others from fighting, he should first notify them of his intention to prevent a breach of the peace.[84]

§ 150. **Hue and Cry.** — It was formerly the law in England, by Statute 13 Edward I, Chapter 3, that every hundred (a division of a county)[85] was

---

[82] Lott v. Sweet, 33 Mich. 308; Paetz v. Dain, Wils. (Ind.) 148.

[83] Handcock v. Baker, 2 B. & P. (Eng. C. P.) 260; Selw. 3d ed. 830; Bacon's Abr. Trespass, D 3.

[84] 1 East P. C. 304; Bacon's Abr. Trespass, D 3; 2 Rolles Abr. 559.

[85] Regan v. N. Y. etc. R R. Co., 60 Conn. 124. In Delaware the sub-divisions of a county are called "hundreds." They correspond to "towns," in New England; "townships," in New Jersey, and "parishes" in Louisiana.

bound to answer for all robberies therein committed, unless they took the felon.[86] For that reason it was common to make fresh pursuit, with hue and cry, by both horsemen and footmen,[87] of one who had committed a felony. These acts are now repealed, and an arrest by hue and cry is seldom known. Of the same effect, however, in later usage, is a written proclamation issued on the escape of a felon from prison, requiring all persons to aid in retaking him.

[86] Grosvenor *v.* Inhab. etc. of St. Augustine, 12 East, 244.
[87] Made imperative by Stat. 27 Eliz. c. 13.

CHAPTER VII

BREAKING DOORS TO MAKE AN ARREST

§ 151. **Man's Habitation is Sacred.** — The law regards a man's house as his castle, his place of refuge, his sanctuary, and is predisposed to protect it against forcible invasion and disturbance. This protection is afforded, not only because of man's natural right of undisturbed habitation, which nature has ever impelled him to maintain, even when in a savage state, but also because of the terror which usually results from an invasion of this right, and the possibility of such invasion causing a breach of the peace through being met with resistance.

§ 152. **Breaking into Dwelling-house to serve Process.** — As a result of this tender regard of the law for the habitation of man, it is well settled that an outer door or window of a dwelling-house cannot be broken to execute civil process. In the execution of criminal process, however, the law, with due regard for the well-settled principle " individual rights yield to public necessity," allows the habitation of man to be entered forcibly under certain conditions.[1]

---

[1] Com. v. Reynolds, 120 Mass. 190; Shanley v. Wells, 71 Ill. 78; Cahill v. People, 106 Ill. 621; State v. Smith, 1 N. H. 346.

§ 153. **Notification, Demand, and Refusal are Necessary.** — To serve a criminal process a dwelling-house may be forcibly entered by an officer after a proper notification of the purpose of the entry, and a demand upon the inmates to open the house, and a refusal by them to do so.[2] And even if it appeared that the defendant was not in the house at the time such arrest was attempted to be made, yet the breaking and entering the house for the purpose of arresting him would be justified, if the officer acted in good faith, under reasonable belief that the party was there,[3] and after proper notice broke and entered the house, doing no unnecessary violence or damage;[4] and such is the law even though the offence for which the warrant was issued is but a misdemeanor.[5]

§ 154. **Name of Party sought need not be given unless requested.** — It is not necessary to notify

---

[2] Barnard v. Bartlett, 10 Cush. (Mass.) 501; McLennon v. Richardson, 15 Gray (Mass.), 74; State v. Oliver, 2 Houst. (Del.) 585; Semayne's Case, 5 Coke (Eng. K. B.), 91 b; Lannock v. Brown, 2 B. & Ald. (Eng. K. B.) 592; Read v. Case, 4 Conn. 166.

[3] Com. v. Irwin, 1 Allen (Mass.), 587.

[4] Com. v. Reynolds, 120 Mass. 190; Com. v. Irwin, supra cit.

[5] Com. v. Reynolds, supra cit.; State v. Shaw, 1 Root (Conn.), 134; State v. Mooring, 115 N. C. 709; State v. Oliver, 2 Houst. (Del.) 585; U. S. v. Faw, 1 Cranch (U. S. C. C.), 487. *Contra:* Com. v. County Prison, 5 Pa. Dist. 635.

the occupier of the house who the person sought to be arrested is, if no inquiry is made in relation thereto, even if the person sought to be arrested is not actually in the house, it being sufficient for the occupier to know that an officer, provided with a warrant against an alleged offender, who believes that he is within his house, is seeking to arrest him there.[6]

§ 155. **Private Person's Right to break Doors.** — Any private person who is present when any felony is committed, is bound to arrest the felon, and may break open doors when following him in fresh pursuit upon reliable information.[7] But a private person is not justified in breaking doors to arrest a person upon a groundless suspicion, no matter how reasonable or well founded his suspicion may be.[8]

§ 156. **To whom the Protection of the Dwelling-house is extended.** — A dwelling-house cannot be forced by an officer in the execution of civil process against the occupier or any of his family who have their domicil or ordinary residence there; and this immunity from arrest extends not only to the occupant, his wife and children, but to domestic servants, and permanent boarders and lodgers as well, but not to strangers or visitors.[9] So that if a

---

[6] Com. v. Reynolds, 120 Mass. 190.
[7] Brooks v. Com., 61 Pa. St. 352.
[8] Ibid.
[9] Oystead v. Shed, 13 Mass. 520.

stranger whose ordinary residence is elsewhere, upon a pursuit, take refuge in the house of another, the house is not *his* castle; and the officer may break open the doors or windows in order to execute his process.

If the occupant should refuse admission to the officer *after his purpose and authority were made known*, the law would consider him as conspiring with the party pursued to screen him from arrest, and would not allow him to make his house a place of refuge.[10]

§ 157. **Breaking into Dwelling-house to prevent Escape.** — It would be different, however, if the occupier of a house was arrested outside of his house, and then fled to his house for protection. In such case the officer would have a clear right to pursue and break into the house, for he would not then be effecting an arrest, but would be preventing an escape. But the breaking will not be justified unless the arrest outside the house was absolutely complete.[11]

§ 158. **Arrest within House by Officer Outside.** — Where one is arrested by the officer touching him for the purpose of arresting him, through a broken window,[12] the arrest having been consummated by the touching of the defendant, the officer

[10] Oystead *v.* Shed, 13 Mass. 520.
[11] See Chapter IV. as to acts completing arrest.
[12] Sandow *v.* Jervis, E. B. & E. (Eng. Q. B.) 935, 942.

may break an outer door, not to execute the civil process, for that was executed by the act of arrest, but to remove his prisoner.

§ 159. **Unannounced Breaking to make Original Arrest not justified.** — It was decided as early as 1605,[13] that the householder must be requested to open the door before the officer can break his way in; and such is still the law.[14] In fact it is necessary (1) that the officer give notice of his purpose and his authority, (2) demand admission, and (3) be refused admission, before he can break a door or window of a dwelling-house to make an arrest on either a civil or a criminal process.

§ 160. **Breaking may be unannounced if Arrest is following Escape.** — But if a person who has been arrested escapes, and takes refuge in the house of another, the officer may break into such other person's house to retake him; and if the pursuit is fresh, so that the occupant is consequently aware of the object of the officer, no notice of purpose, demand of admission, and refusal to admit is necessary to justify the officer in breaking the outer door.[15]

§ 161. **Officer may re-enter Forcibly if Necessary.** — If an officer has once been lawfully in the

[13] Semayne v. Gresham, 5 Coke (Eng. K. B.), 91.
[14] Barnard v. Bartlett, 10 Cush. (Mass.) 501; Com. v. Reynolds, 120 Mass. 190.
[15] Allen v. Martin, 10 Wend. (N. Y.) 300.

house in making an arrest on civil process, he may re-enter, using as much force as may be necessary.[16] So where an officer obtained a peaceable entrance through an outer door, and before he could make an arrest was forcibly ejected from the house, and the door fastened against him, he was justified in forcing open the door, without a demand of re-admittance, and making the arrest.[17]

§ 162. **Inner Doors may be broken on any Process.** — While the law prohibits the breaking of the outer door of a dwelling-house to execute civil process, it does not extend the protection to the inner doors,[18] except where an inner door is the entrance to a distinct apartment,[19] or to the outer doors or windows of other buildings not the dwelling of the debtor.[20]

§ 163. **When Usual Inner Door is a Legal Outer Door.** — Where a house is let to lodgers, the owner retaining one room thereof for himself, an officer may break open an inner door which leads to the owner's room, for the purpose of arresting him.[21]

But if the whole house be let in lodgings, as each lodging is then considered a dwelling-house, in which burglary may be stated to have been com-

[16] Genner *v.* Sparks, 6 Mod. (Eng. K. B. &c.) 173.
[17] Aga Kurhboolie Mahomed *v.* Reg., 3 Moore, P. C. (Eng.) 164.
[18] Hubbard *v.* Mace, 17 Johns. (N. Y.) 127.
[19] Stedman *v.* Crane, 11 Metc. (Mass.) 295.
[20] Haggerty *v.* Wilber, 16 Johns. (N. Y.) 287.
[21] Williams *v.* Spencer, 5 Johns. (N. Y.) 352.

mitted, it has been supposed that the door of each apartment would be considered an outer door which could not be legally broken open to execute a civil arrest.[22]

What is a Dwelling-House?

§ 164. **Definition.** — A dwelling-house is a building inhabited by man. A house usually occupied by the person there residing and his family.[23]

§ 165. **Use determines Character.** — The use to which a house is put, at the time of the offence, determines its character.[24] A barn may be converted into a dwelling-house, or a dwelling-house into a barn, by a change of its uses.[25] A cabin in the woods, built as a permanent structure for wood-choppers to occupy, is a dwelling-house if in actual use as a place of abode.[26]

A house merely designed as a dwelling-house, but not occupied for that purpose, is not a dwelling-house.[27]

§ 166. **Use of Portion as Dwelling.** — It is not necessary that the entire building be used as a dwelling-place, to make the entire building a dwell-

---

[22] Oystead v. Shed, 13 Mass. 519.
[23] Bouvier's Law Dict. (Dwelling-house).
[24] State v. Williams, 40 W. Va. 268; Davis v. State, 38 Ohio St. 506.
[25] Davis v. State, supra cit.
[26] State v. Weber, 156 Mo. 257.
[27] State v. Warren, 33 Me. 30.

ing-house. If part of a building is used as a place of abode, every part of the building to which there is an internal communication from the part used as a dwelling is part of the dwelling-house. Thus the loft of a coach-house and stable which is used as the dwelling of the coachman is his dwelling-house, although the principal use of the building is that of a coach-house and stable.[28]

§ 167. **May be Several Dwellings in same Building.** — Where a building is leased to different persons in distinct apartments, each apartment is the dwelling-house of the lessee.[29]

§ 168. **Public Building may be a Dwelling.** — A suite of rooms in a college is a dwelling-house.[30] So is a public jail,[31] or an infirmary.[32] And a building thirty-six feet distant from the main dwelling, in which the servants sleep, is a part of the dwelling-house.[33]

§ 169. **Combined Residence and Place of Business.** — Where the front of a building is occupied by the owner as a shoe-shop, and is connected with the rear and overhead portion, which is used as a dwelling, the building is a dwelling-house.[34]

[28] Rex v. Turner, 1 Leach (Eng. C. C.), 305.
[29] Stedman v. Crane, 11 Metc. (Mass.) 295.
[30] Barnes v. Peters, L. R. 4 C. P. 539.
[31] People v. Cowteral, 18 Johns. (N. Y.) 115.
[32] Davis v. State, 38 Ohio St. 506.
[33] Pond v. People, 8 Mich. 150.
[34] People v. Dupree, 98 Mich. 26.

And where a woman occupied as her dwelling a building containing a single room, in which she also carried on her trade as a milliner, and kept therein a stock of millinery goods, it was held that the use of the room as a place of business did not change its character as a dwelling, and that breaking the door in the execution of civil process was illegal.[35]

§ 170. **Use of House must be Primarily and Habitually for Sleeping Purposes.** — The house must be used as the usual and habitual place for sleeping purposes, by the owner or some member of his family, or his servants, in order to make it a dwelling-house.

A storehouse of the owner, who resides nearby, and in which he *occasionally* slept, is not a dwelling-house.[36] But if a part of a storehouse, communicating with the part used for store purposes, is slept in *habitually* by the owner or some member of his family, although he sleeps there for the purpose of protecting the premises, it is his dwelling-house. If, however, the person who sleeps there is not the owner, or one of his family, or a servant, or clerk, but is employed to sleep there *solely* for the purpose of protecting the premises, the store is not a dwelling-house.[37]

[35] Welsh *v.* Wilson, 34 Minn. 92.
[36] State *v.* Jenkins, 5 Jones (N. C.), 430.
[37] State *v.* Potts, 75 N. C. 129; State *v.* Williams, 90 N. C. 724.

§ 171. **Effect of Absence.** — A house which the owner visits once or twice a year, and at each visit sleeps there for about a week, at other times the house being unoccupied, is not a dwelling-house except when so occupied.[38] But a temporary absence with the intention of returning does not make a building lose its character as a dwelling-house.[39]

What is a Breaking?

§ 172. **Same in Serving Process as in Burglary.** — What would be a "breaking" of the outer door in burglary is equally a breaking by the sheriff when he enters to make a levy,[40] or when he, or any other officer, comes to serve any legal process.

§ 173. **Does not Necessarily involve Injury of Material.** — "Breaking" does not mean that any part of the material used in the construction of a door, or window, or any other part of the house must be actually broken or even injured. If anything material which constitutes a part of the dwelling-house, and is relied on as a security against intrusion, be broken, removed, or put aside, there is a breaking.[41]

§ 174. **Taking Advantage of Negligence of Occupant.** — But if the occupant of a house is negli-

---

[38] Scott v. State, 62 Miss. 781.

[39] Harrison v. State, 74 Ga. 801; Schwabacher v. People, 165 Ill. 618; Ex parte Vincent, 26 Ala. 145.

[40] Curtis v. Hubbard, 1 Hill (N. Y.) 338.

[41] State v. Boon, 35 N. C. 244 ; Walker v. State, 52 Ala. 376.

gent, and does not avail himself of the usual methods of protecting his dwelling, then one who takes advantage of his negligence is not guilty of breaking.[42]

§ 175. **Breaking Doors.** — Opening a door by lifting the latch,[43] or by turning the knob of a closed door is, in law, a complete breaking.[44] Or opening a door by unhooking a chain which is hooked over a nail,[45] or to push open a door which is entirely closed, but which is neither locked nor latched, is a sufficient breaking.[46] So where a door was made in two sections, upper and lower, the upper section being open, it is a breaking to unhook the lower door; and the fact that the upper door was open, so that the party might have entered without unfastening the lower door, makes no legal difference in the entry.[47] And where a screen door, entirely closed, was pushed open, although the permanent door was not closed, it was held a breaking.[48]

[42] State *v.* Henry, 9 Ired. (N. C.) 463; Rex *v.* Spriggs, 1 Mood. & Rob. (Eng. N. P.) 357.

[43] State *v.* Groning, 33 Kan. 18; State *v.* O'Brien, 81 Iowa, 93; Hedrick *v.* State, 40 Tex. Cr. 532; State *v.* Boon, 35 N. C. 244; Tickner *v.* People, 6 Hun (N. Y.), 657; State *v.* Hecox, 83 Mo. 531; Bass *v.* State, 69 Tenn. 444; McCourt *v.* People, 64 N. Y. 583.

[44] Walker *v.* State, 52 Ala. 376.

[45] State *v.* Hecox, 83 Mo. 531.

[46] State *v.* Reid, 20 Iowa, 413; State *v.* Groning, 33 Kan. 18.

[47] Ferguson *v.* State, 52 Neb. 432.

[48] State *v.* Conners, 95 Iowa, 485.

The removing of a post leaning against a door to keep it closed also constitutes a breaking.[49] And the outer door being shut, is equally a protection whether the owner or possessor be within at the time or not.[50] Raising a trap door which is held in place by its own weight is also a breaking.[51]

§ 176. **Breaking Windows.** — And it is a breaking within the meaning of the law even to push open a swinging transom window, which is not fastened, but is kept in place merely by its own weight,[52] or raising an unfastened window,[53] or removing a window screen that is fastened with nails,[54] or any other window covering, even if held in place by its weight alone.

§ 177. **Entering other Openings.** — Entering by means of a chimney[55] is a breaking, because this is an opening which necessarily exists in order that the building may be occupied as a dwelling-house.

[49] State v. Powell, 61 Kan. 81; State v. Woods, 137 Mo. 6; Matthews v. State, 38 S. W. (Tex.) 172.

[50] Curtis v. Hubbard, 1 Hill (N. Y.), 338.

[51] Harrison v. State, 20 Tex. App. 387; Carter v. State, 68 Ala. 96.

[52] Dennis v. People, 27 Mich. 151; Timmons v. State, 34 Ohio St. 426.

[53] State v. Boon, 35 N. C. 244; Frank v. State, 39 Miss. 705; Rex v. Hyams, 7 C. & P. (Eng. N. P.) 441.

[54] Com. v. Stephenson, 8 Pick. (Mass.) 354; Sims v. State, 136 Ind. 358.

[55] Rex v. Brice, Russ. & Ry. (Eng. C. C.) 450; Walker v. State, 52 Ala. 376.

But it seems that it is not a breaking to enter through a hole in the roof of a house, left there for the purpose of giving light,[56] because the owner might have protected his premises by covering the opening with a fastened window; or to enter by a door or window which is already partly opened, although the opening may be very slight.[57]

In all such cases the negligence of the occupier, in leaving his premises insufficiently protected, reduces an illegal entrance to a mere trespass, without attaching to it a breaking.

§ 178. **Enlarging Opening by Actual Breaking.** — But where an opening is enlarged by an actual breaking of material, or even where a broken window-pane, still entirely in place, is removed so as to effect an entrance, or the breaking or pushing in of a part of a pane of glass which had been previously cut, but the whole of which still remained in its place,[58] is a sufficient breaking.

So where a hole is dug under a building made of logs, which has no floor except the ground, there is a breaking.[59]

§ 179. **Mere Protective Doors are not "Outer" Doors.** — Where there are two doors to the cellarway of a dwelling-house, one opening outwardly,

---

[56] Rex v. Spriggs, 1 Mood. & Rob. (Eng. N. P.) 357.
[57] Com. v. Strupney, 105 Mass. 588.
[58] Reg. v. Bird, 9 C. & P. (Eng. N. P.) 44.
[59] Pressley v. State, 111 Ala. 34.

and the other opening into the cellar, the latter is the outer door of the house, and if closed and latched, the unlatching and entering constitutes a breaking.[60] Upon like reasoning the storm-door is not the outer door of a house.[61]

§ 180. **Removal of Iron Grating over Sidewalk.** — One decision apparently in conflict with the last cited case is, that the removal of an iron grating over the sidewalk, for the purpose of effecting an entrance through a cellar window into the building, is a breaking.[62] But in this case it seems that the cellar window was left open by the owner, who apparently relied upon the grating to protect the building against intruders, and this allows the cases to be reconciled.

§ 181. **Entrance by Means of Deception.** — To gain an entrance by deception, as where the officer announced that he had a note for the party whose arrest was sought,[63] or that he wanted to see some other person who was in the house, and thereby gained admission,[64] have been held legal entrances, although such entrances in the law of burglary are held breakings.[65] And it was held that where the

[60] McCourt v. People, 64 N. Y. 583.
[61] Ibid.
[62] People v. Nolan, 22 Mich. 229.
[63] Rex v. Backhouse, Lofft (Eng. K. B.), 61.
[64] Hitchcock v. Holmes, 43 Conn. 528.
[65] Johnston v. Com., 85 Pa. St. 54.

occupant of a house, decoyed therefrom by the stratagem of the trespasser, left his door unfastened, and fifteen minutes later the trespasser entered the unfastened door, there was no breaking, by reason of the negligence of the remaining members of the family not fastening the door during that interval.[66]

But if the occupant is induced to open the door by threats, or if the officer claims that he is coming to serve a different sort of a process, and by his false statement procures an entrance, there would be a breaking.

§ 182. **Effect of Illegal Breaking on the Arrest.** — An arrest of a person in a civil action, by an unlawful breaking, not only subjects the officer to a civil action for the trespass, but the arrest is altogether void.[67] In a criminal action, however, the illegality of the arrest of one before the court on a valid criminal charge will not be considered in that case.[68]

[66] State *v.* Henry, 9 Ired. (N. C.) 463.
[67] Kerbey *v.* Denbey, 1 M. & W. (Eng. Exch.) 336.
[68] Com. *v.* Conlin, 184 Mass. 195.

CHAPTER VIII

FORCE IN THE ACT OF ARREST

§ 183. Authority and Duty are Coincident. — The law never clothes a person with authority to make an arrest without, at the same time, placing upon him the *duty* of making it.

In the discharge of this duty, the arresting party may use all the force that is absolutely necessary to effect the arrest, even under some circumstances to the point of killing; but the use of unnecessary force can never be justified.

The law deprecates the necessity of killing a human being in the act of making an arrest, and will not allow either the party making the arrest, or the party whose arrest is desired, in case of a wanton abuse of right, to shield himself behind a technicality of law.

So that, while there are cases holding that the taking of life by the officer, or by the accused, or by a private party in a case wherein he may lawfully act, is justifiable under certain circumstances, these cases may not always be safely relied upon to protect the party who does the killing.

This is largely true by reason of the different views held by the people of different parts of the country respecting the amount of provocation that will justify a homicide, — the killing of a human being by a human being. And it is always the people — the jury — of the place where the homicide occurs that are to say whether the killing is to be sanctioned or punished, and whether the officer acted on reasonable grounds.[1] Hence, a case decided in a community where verbal or written insults and provocations are held, under certain conditions, to justify a killing, is not a safe precedent for one to rely on in a community where mere words, no matter how strongly inclined to arouse man's passions, are held never to justify a homicide. In fact, with the advancement of legal attainments, and general enlightenment of society, the occasions where the taking of human life may be justified by one enforcing legal arrest, or resisting illegal arrest, are becoming fewer.

§ 184. **Blackstone's Rule not Reliable.** — Blackstone wrote, about 1769, that a crime might be prevented by death if the same, if committed, would be punished by death. But this rule does not now hold good, because at that time all felonies were punishable by death, whereas now but few are so punishable; while in some States the death penalty is altogether abolished.

§ 185. **Officer may use all Necessary Force.** — It may be said that an officer whose duty it is to make

[1] State v. Bland, 97 N. C. 438.

an arrest may use all force that is necessary in making the arrest, even to the point of taking life,[2] *when there is no other way of making the arrest*, and it makes no difference whether the process is civil or criminal.[3]

§ 186. **May not use Unnecessary Force.** — But it is his duty to use no unnecessary harshness or violence;[4] and if he use more force than is necessary, he himself becomes liable in trespass,[5] and in case of taking life may be guilty of manslaughter, or even murder,[6] according to the degree of wanton-

---

[2] State v. Dierberger, 96 Mo. 666; Brooks v. Com., 61 Pa. St. 352; Head v. Martin, 85 Ky. 480; Mesmer v. Com., 26 Gratt. (Va.) 976; State v. Miller, 5 Ohio Dec. 703; Shovlin v. Com., 106 Pa. St. 369; James v. State, 44 Tex. 314; Golden v. State, 1 S. C. 292; State v. Sigman, 106 N. C. 728; Patterson v. State, 91 Ala. 58; Ramsey v. State, 92 Ga. 53; Murdock v. Ripley, 35 Me. 472; State v. Lafferty, 5 Harr. (Del.) 491; People v. Durfee, 62 Mich. 487; State v. Fuller, 96 Mo. 165; People v. Carlton, 115 N. Y. 618; U. S. v. Fullhart, 47 Fed. Rep. (U. S.) 802.

[3] Clements v. State, 50 Ala. 117.

[4] Fulton v. Staats, 41 N. Y. 498; North v. People, 139 Ill. 81; Findlay v. Pruitt, 9 Port. (Ala.) 195; Lander v. Miles, 3 Oreg. 35; Burns v. State, 80 Ga. 544; State v. Pate, 7 Ohio N. P. 543; Reneau v. State, 2 Lea (Tenn.), 720; State v. Mahon, 3 Harr. (Del.) 568; Skidmore v. State, 43 Tex. 93.

[5] Murdock v. Ripley, 35 Me. 472; Golden v. State, 1 S. C. 292; Patterson v. State, 91 Ala. 58; Dilger v. Com., 88 Ky. 550.

[6] Williams v. State, 44 Ala. 41; State v. Bryant, 65 N. C. 327; Reneau v. State, 2 Lea (Tenn.), 720; State v. Dietz, 59 Kan. 576.

ness and recklessness of human life manifested in the homicide.

If no resistance be offered, or attempt to escape, he has no right, rudely and with violence, to seize and collar his prisoner.[7]

§ 187. **May use Force to prevent Escape. — Felony.** — Any force which may be used to effect an arrest may also be used to prevent an escape and retain custody of the prisoner, and an officer attempting to arrest a person guilty of a felony, at least of the more atrocious kind, may kill to prevent an escape either before or after the arrest when there is no other way of preventing it.[8]

It has been wisely held that this doctrine does not apply to all felonies, but only to those of a more atrocious kind, as rape and murder; therefore it was held that one was not justified in shooting to prevent the escape of one who had stolen a hog.[9]

§ 188. **Misdemeanor.** — With much stronger reason would the right to kill not exist in preventing an escape in case of a misdemeanor;[10] such killing

[7] State *v.* Mahon, 3 Harr. (Del.) 568.
[8] 1 Hale's P. C. 481; 4 Bl. Com. 293; Jackson *v.* State, 66 Miss. 89.
[9] State *v.* Bryant, 65 N. C. 327.
[10] Tiner *v.* State, 44 Tex. 128; Williams *v.* State, 44 Ala. 41; Thomas *v.* Kinkead, 55 Ark. 502; Head *v.* Martin, 85 Ky. 480; Rischer *v.* Meehan, 11 Ohio C. C. 403; U. S. *v.*

would be murder.[11] And it has been held that an officer has no right, when endeavoring to execute a warrant on a bastardy charge, to shoot the accused when fleeing, either to effect his arrest or to prevent his escape.[12] A party guilty of a misdemeanor, fired upon by an officer while avoiding arrest, may repel the attack by shooting the officer, and the killing will not necessarily be unlawful.[13]

§ 189. **Fleeing from Arrest.** — There is a broad distinction between resisting arrest and the avoidance of it; between forcible opposition to arrest and merely fleeing from it; and there is no rule of law that he who flees from attempted arrest in case of misdemeanor thereby forfeits his right to defend his life.[14]

Even in case of one charged with murder, so long as the one sought to be arrested was content peaceably to avoid arrest, the pursuing party had no right to kill him; but whenever, by his conduct, he puts

Clark, 31 Fed. Rep. (U.S.) 710; Brown v. Weaver, 76 Miss. 7; Conraddy v. People, 5 Park. Cr. (N. Y.) 234; Reneau v. State, 2 Lea (Tenn.), 720; Forster's Case, 1 Lewin (Eng. C. C.), 187; Handley v. State, 96 Ala. 48; Com. v. Green, 20 Pa. Co. Ct. 535; Dilger v. Com., 88 Ky. 550; Wright v. State, 44 Tex. 645. *Contra:* State v. Dierberger, 96 Mo. 666.

[11] Reneau v. State, 2 Lea (Tenn.), 720; State v. Dietz, 59 Kan. 576.
[12] Head v. Martin, 85 Ky. 480.
[13] Tiner v. State, 44 Tex. 128.
[14] Ibid.

in jeopardy the life of any attempting to arrest him, he may be killed, and the act will be excusable.[15]

§ 190. **Officer is liable for Excessive Force.** — In any case, a felon must not be killed in endeavoring to effect his capture, if the officer can arrest him without such severity, by obtaining assistance, or otherwise, of which the jury ought to inquire.[16]

The amount of force which an officer may lawfully use in making an arrest is so much as is necessary to accomplish his object; and where he is charged with exceeding that limit, the jury must judge of the necessity and not the officer.[17] If the amount used is more than the occasion requires, he is criminally liable for the excess.[18] So where a police officer is endeavoring to arrest a drunken cab driver, he has no right to strike him with his club in such a manner as to break his arm, and an indictment will lie for the assault and battery.[19]

And where an officer makes an arrest of an offender, whom he finds taking a meal at a public hotel, by

[15] State *v.* Anderson, 1 Hill (S. C.), 327.
[16] Williams *v.* State, 44 Ala. 41.
[17] State *v.* Bland, 97 N. C. 438.
[18] Patterson *v.* State, 91 Ala. 58; State *v.* Fuller, 96 Mo. 165; State *v.* Lafferty, 5 Harr. (Del.) 491; Golden *v.* State, 1 S. C. 292; State *v.* Mahon, 3 Harr. (Del.) 568; Mesmer *v.* Com., 26 Gratt. (Va.) 976; Ramsey *v.* State, 92 Ga. 53; Beaverts *v.* State, 4 Tex. App. 175; Mockabee *v.* Com., 78 Ky. 380; Murdock *v.* Ripley, 35 Me. 472; Bowling *v.* Com., 7 Ky. L. 821; Dilger *v.* Com., 88 Ky. 550.
[19] Golden *v.* State, 1 S. C. 292.

rudely seizing him and throwing him violently to the floor, then striking him with the butt of his pistol and knocking him senseless, no evidence having been adduced to show occasion for use of such force, the officer was properly found guilty of assault.[20]

§ 191. **Officer's Right to use Club.** — Where an officer whose duty it was on a public occasion to see that a passage was kept for the passing of vehicles, directed a person in front of the crowd to stand back, and on being told by him that he could not for those behind him, struck him immediately on the face, without any other effort to remove him, saying that he would make him stand back, it was held that the officer exceeded his authority and should have confined himself to pressure.[21]

Where an officer finds two persons fighting, and, grasping one by the shoulder, tells him that he is under arrest, if the prisoner still continues to strike at his opponent, the officer may be justified in striking him with his club in order to stop the fight, if he uses no unnecessary force in doing so.[22]

But an officer is not justified in striking one with his club who interferes with him in the performance of his duty, although he would be justified in placing him under arrest.[23] Nor has an officer

---

[20] Beaverts v. State, 4 Tex. App. 175.
[21] Imason v. Cope, 5 C. & P. (Eng. N. P.) 193.
[22] State v. Pugh, 101 N. C. 737.
[23] Levy v. Edwards, 1 C. & P. (Eng. N. P.) 40.

the right to strike with his club one who merely holds back, and is not otherwise resisting.[24]

§ 192. **Demanding Officer's Number.** — Any citizen has a right to demand of a police officer his number, and the demanding of the number of an officer is no crime, nor is the temporarily standing in front of him for that purpose. And where a party remonstrates with an officer for making an arrest, or demands his number, he is not guilty of obstructing an officer.[25] But if the remonstrance be carried to a point where the prisoner is incited to resist, there will be an offence,[26] for which the officer may arrest the inciting party.[27]

§ 193. **Officer's Unlawful Act deprives him of Protection.** — If an officer has brought peril upon himself by his own unlawful act, either in making the arrest, or in the treatment of his prisoner while under arrest, he will not be justified in taking the life of his prisoner on the ground of self-defence.[28]

And if there is no attempt to escape, and no forcible resistance, it is an excess of authority and a criminal offence, which may well be called an outrage in an officer, to inflict any blow or other violence upon his prisoner; and the prisoner is

---

[24] Com. v. Weathers, 7 Kulp (Pa.), 1.
[25] Com. v. The Sheriff, 3 Brewst. (Pa.) 343.
[26] Ibid.
[27] White v. Edmunds, 1 Peake (Eng. N. P.), 89.
[28] Com. v. Weathers, 7 Kulp (Pa.), 1.

justified in using any force not excessive in defending himself from the unauthorized assault.[29]

§ 193 a. Officer detailed as Guard. — Where an officer is detailed to protect a judge or other person, it is his duty to see that no harm comes to the person under his charge; and if the circumstances are such that he may reasonably believe that killing of a person attempting to assault the one under his care is necessary for the safety of his charge, he is justified in taking the life of the assailant.[30]

§ 194. Use of Handcuffs. — Because an officer is responsible for the safe-keeping of his prisoner, and may become liable either civilly or criminally for his escape, the law leaves the question of necessity in the use of handcuffs largely to the discretion of the officer, and holds him liable only for a clear abuse of his authority.[31]

So where an officer handcuffed one charged with a misdemeanor to one convicted of a felony, and walked them thus together through the streets, he was held liable for the abuse of his authority.[32]

---

[29] State *v.* Belk, 76 N. C. 10.

[30] In re Neagle, 135 U. S. 1.

[31] Dehm *v.* Hinman, 56 Conn. 320; Wright *v.* Court, 4 B. & C. (Eng. K. B.) 596; Leigh *v.* Cole, 6 Cox C. C. 329; Firestone *v.* Rice, 71 Mich. 377; Cochran *v.* Toher, 14 Minn. 385; State *v.* Stalcup, 24 N. C. 50. But see Giroux *v.* State, 40 Tex. 97.

[32] Leigh *v.* Cole, 6 Cox C. C. (Eng.) 329.

The right to handcuff must depend on the circumstances of each particular case, considering the nature of the charge, and the conduct and temper of the person in custody.[33]

In order to justify an officer in handcuffing a prisoner arrested for a felony, it is not necessary that he should be unruly, or attempt to escape, or to do anything indicating a necessity for such restraint, nor in the absence of these indications that he should be a *notoriously* bad character.[34]

Where friends of the prisoner threaten to release him by force, the officer may be justified in placing his prisoner in irons immediately after the threats are made.[35]

[33] Leigh v. Cole, 6 Cox C. C. (Eng.) 329.
[34] Firestone v. Rice, 71 Mich. 377.
[35] Cochran v. Toher, 14 Minn. 385.

CHAPTER IX

DISPOSING OF THE PRISONER

§ 195. Officer's Duty after Arrest. — After an arrest has been made, the next duty of the arresting party is to have his prisoner before a magistrate,[1] in order that the offence with which the prisoner is charged may be inquired into. To this effect the prisoner may be confined in the most suitable place, for a reasonable time, until it is possible for him to be taken before the magistrate. The length of time during which this confinement may continue lawful will vary according to the circumstances of the case, but it may be laid down as a general rule that it must continue no longer than the exigencies of the case absolutely demand, and any further delay will make the officer guilty of false imprisonment.[2]

§ 196. Unconstitutional Law is no Protection to Officer. — So where a town by-law authorized an officer to arrest and detain without warrant for the space of forty-eight hours, it was held that such

---

[1] See § 96, supra; Kindred *v.* Stitt, 51 Ill. 401.

[2] Burke *v.* Bell, 36 Me. 317; Cochran *v.* Toher, 14 Minn. 385.

law was repugnant to the general law of the State, and therefore void, and that in an action for trespass, the officer could not justify his acts under that law.[3] And where the detention was for five days, it was unreasonable, as a matter of law, and should not have been left to the jury to consider as a matter of fact.[4]

§ 197. **Termination of Officer's Control.** — When an officer has made an arrest under a warrant, his custody of the prisoner does not cease until the prisoner has been discharged, admitted to bail, or committed to jail upon a mittimus issued by the court,[5] and it is his duty to exercise such control over the prisoner that he may not escape until the discharge, admission to bail, or commitment has been secured. When the arrest is without warrant, the officer's custody may cease without taking the prisoner before the magistrate, in certain cases, as where he makes an arrest upon suspicion, and the suspicion subsequently disappears,[6] or where, even in case the statute commands that the officer take his prisoner before the magistrate, the express waiver of this right by the prisoner will justify the officer in discharging him for good reason.[7]

[3] Burke v. Bell, 36 Me. 317.
[4] Cochran v. Toher, 14 Minn. 385.
[5] Com. v. Morihan, 4 Allen (Mass.), 585.
[6] Burke v. Bell, supra cit.
[7] Brock v. Stimson, 108 Mass. 520 ; Phillips v. McFadden, 125 Mass. 198.

§ 198. **Use of Handcuffs.** — To get his prisoner to a suitable place of confinement, or before the magistrate, he may use all force that is reasonably necessary, and he may handcuff his prisoner whenever it may reasonably appear to him to be necessary to do so in order to retain his custody of the prisoner,[8] even though it should subsequently be shown that the act of handcuffing was entirely unnecessary.[9] But an officer who has arrested a defendant in a civil suit, or a person accused of a crime, has no right to handcuff him unless it is reasonably necessary, or he has attempted to make his escape.[10] And, without some good reason, a prisoner must not be brought shackled into court.[11]

§ 199. **Right to take Prisoner through Streets in Scanty Attire.** — If a person legally arrested, even by a private person without a warrant, is not sufficiently attired, and after an opportunity to clothe himself is given him, he refuses to put on clothing, he may be taken, if necessary, through the public street without the usual attire, and delivered thus to the proper authority.[12]

---

[8] Dehm v. Hinman, 56 Conn. 320; State v. Stalcup, 2 Ired. (N. C.) 50.

[9] Firestone v. Rice, 71 Mich. 377.

[10] Wright v. Court, 4 B. & C. (Eng. K. B.) 596.

[11] State v. Kring, 64 Mo. 591; Faire v. State, 58 Ala. 74; People v. Harrington, 42 Cal. 165; Lee v. State, 51 Miss. 566.

[12] Handcock v. Baker, 2 Bos. & Pul. (Eng. Com. Pl.) 260.

§ 200. **Searching the Prisoner.** — An officer has a right to search the prisoner for the purpose of taking from him anything that may be used as evidence in prosecuting him,[13] or anything that may be used by the prisoner in escaping, or to injure either himself or others, but there exists no right to remove from the prisoner his money or any other valuables that may be used by him in providing for his defence.[14]

In an important English case it was said by Justice Patterson: "The prisoner complains that his money was taken from him, and that he was thereby deprived of the means of making his defence. Generally speaking, it is not right that a man's money should be taken away from him, unless it is connected in some way with the property stolen. If it is connected with the robbery, it is quite proper that it should be taken. But unless it is, it is not a fair thing to take away his money which he might use for his defence. I believe constables are too much in the habit of taking away everything they find upon a prisoner, which is certainly not right. And this is a rule which ought

---

[13] Spalding v. Preston, 21 Vt. 9; O'Connor v. Backlin, 59 N. H. 589; Ex parte Hurn, 92 Ala. 102; Reifsnyder v. Lee, 44 Iowa, 101; Dillon v. O'Brien, 16 Cox C. C. (Eng.) 245.

[14] Stuart v. Harris, 69 Ill. App. 668; Rickers v. Simcox, 1 Utah, 33; Hubbard v. Garner, 115 Mich. 406. *Contra:* O'Connor v. Backlin, 59 N. H. 589; Commercial Exch. Bank v. McLeod, 65 Iowa, 665.

to be observed by all policemen and other peace officers."[15]

§ 201. **Removal of Clothing.** — When it becomes necessary to search and take property from the prisoner, all necessary force may be used to accomplish this end,[16] and if necessary the clothing of the prisoner may be removed to complete the search.[17]

§ 202. **Search may be made at Time of Arrest.** — An officer, at the time of making an arrest, may be justified in searching his prisoner, to protect himself. The mere fact that the prisoner is drunk and disorderly will not justify a searching, but a prisoner may, by violent language and conduct, make such search a reasonable and prudent proceeding.[18]

§ 203. **Compulsory Physical Examination.** — The right to search does not give the right to make a compulsory physical examination for the purpose of obtaining evidence.[19]

The right to one's person may be said to be a right of complete immunity, — to be let alone;[20] and further, it has been held that to subject the

[15] Rex v. O'Donnell, 7 C. & P. (Eng. N. P.) 138.
[16] Dillon v. O'Brien, 16 Cox C. C. (Eng.) 245.
[17] Woolfolk v. State, 81 Ga. 551.
[18] Leigh v. Cole, 6 Cox C. C. (Eng.) 329.
[19] People v. McCoy, 45 How. Pr. (N. Y.) 216; Agnew v. Jobson, 13 Cox C. C. (Eng.) 625; Blackwell v. State, 67 Ga. 76.
[20] Cooley on Torts, p. 29.

prisoner to a physical examination against his will, is a violation of the spirit of the Constitution of the United States, Article V, Amendment, which declares that no person shall, in any criminal case, be compelled to be a witness against himself.[21]

But an officer may compel the accused to put his foot into a footprint found at the place where the crime was committed, and at the trial testify to the result of the comparison,[22] or compel the accused to exhibit tattoo marks on his arm for the purpose of identification.[23]

And where the prisoner, charged with homicide, alleged that her hand, which she had wrapped in bandages, had been burned in her endeavor to put out the fire upon the deceased, she was compelled to unwrap it and show it to a physician, and the examination was held justifiable.[24]

[21] People *v.* McCoy, 45 How. Pr. (N. Y.) 216.
[22] State *v.* Graham, 74 N. C. 646.
[23] State *v.* Ah Chuey, 14 Nev. 79.
[24] State *v.* Garrett, 71 N. C. 85.

CHAPTER X

ARREST IN EXTRADITION PROCEEDINGS

§ 204. **Extradition and Rendition distinguished.** — The process of demanding and giving up fugitives from justice, if between nations, is called extradition; if between States of the same nation, is called rendition, although it is very usual to term the process of demanding and giving up fugitives from justice "extradition," whether between States or nations.

§ 205. **Extradition. — Definition.** — Extradition is the surrender by one sovereign State to another, on its demand, of persons charged with the commission of crime within its jurisdiction, that they may be dealt with according to its laws.[1]

§ 206. **Matter of Comity.** — Except under the provisions of treaties, the delivery by one country to another, of fugitives from justice, is a matter of comity, and not of obligation;[2] and a State of the United States cannot regulate the surrender of

---

[1] Bouvier's Law Dict. (Extradition).
[2] U. S. *v.* Raucher, 119 U. S. 407.

fugitives from justice to foreign countries, for that province belongs solely to the Federal government.[3]

§ 207. **Authority for Issue of Warrant.** — A warrant for an arrest in an extradition proceeding may issue under authority of sections 5270-5280 of the Revised Statutes of the United States, and under the provisions of the Constitution of the United States, Article IV, Amendment.

§ 208. **Magistrates designated.** — The magistrates authorized by the Revised Statutes, section 5270, to issue such warrants, are the justices of the Supreme Court, circuit judges, district judges, any commissioner authorized by any court of the United States, or a judge of a court of general jurisdiction of any State.

§ 209. **Requisites of Warrant.** — The requirements respecting complaint, oath, and of the warrant itself, are the same as those respecting ordinary warrants. It need not be accompanied by the indictment or affidavit upon which it is based.[4]

The warrant must show on its face that the magistrate issuing it is one authorized to act in extradition cases.[5] Such warrant is void, unless it shows

---

[3] People v. Curtis, 50 N. Y. 321.
[4] Ex parte Stanley, 25 Tex. App. 372; People v. Donahue, 84 N. Y. 438.
[5] In re Ferez, 7 Blatchf. (U. S. C. C.) 35.

on its face that a requisition has been made under the authority of the foreign government, on the government of the United States, and the authority of the latter government obtained, to apprehend such fugitive.[6] It should also state the offence charged, which must be an offence named in the treaty of extradition. It runs throughout the United States.[7]

§ 210. **Re-arrest after Discharge on Habeas Corpus.** — If an alleged fugitive be discharged on a writ of *habeas corpus*, he may be immediately re-arrested on a new complaint and warrant.[8]

§ 211. **Taking before a Magistrate.** — Upon an arrest in an extradition proceeding, the alleged fugitive from justice is to be brought before the official issuing the warrant so that evidence of his criminality may be considered. The degree of evidence must be such that according to the laws of the place where the fugitive is found, it would justify his apprehension and commitment for trial if the crime or offence had been committed there.

§ 212. **Delivery of Fugitive to Demanding State.** — If the magistrate deems the evidence sufficient, he will certify the same, together with a copy of the testimony taken before him, to the Secretary of

[6] In re Ferez, 7 Blatchf. (U. S. C. C.) 35.
[7] In re Heinrich, 5 Blatchf. (U. S. C. C.) 414.
[8] In re Macdonnell, 11 Blatchf. (U. S. C. C.) 170.

State, and commit the prisoner to jail until the surrender be made, which must be within two calendar months. The Secretary of State will then, upon proper demand being made by the foreign government, order, under his hand and seal of office, in the name and by the authority of the President, the person so committed to be delivered to such person as may be authorized in the name and on behalf of such foreign government to receive him.

§ 213. **Scope of Habeas Corpus Writ.** — A fugitive about to be returned to the State from which he fled should be allowed enough time to apply for a writ of *habeas corpus,* in the State of his asylum. But on a writ of *habeas corpus* the guilt or innocence of the prisoner will not be inquired into, for that is exclusively within the province of the courts of the demanding State.[9] The only matters to be inquired into on such writ are whether the proceedings for the extradition have been regular and in compliance with the Constitution and laws of the United States.

§ 214. **Negotiations must be by Highest Executive Officials.** — There can be no extradition or rendition without a demand by the highest executive authority in the State from which the fugitive from justice has fled, upon the highest executive author-

---

[9] In re Sheldon, 34 Ohio St. 319 ; In re White, 55 Fed. Rep. (U. S.) 54 ; Ex parte Devine, 74 Miss. 715.

ity of the State in which the fugitive is asylumed. And a warrant to arrest a fugitive in the harboring State must be issued only upon sanction and order of the highest executive official, — the chief magistrate of that State.[10] The judiciary of the United States possess no jurisdiction in matters of extradition until a demand has been thus made and sanctioned.

§ 215. **Method of Procedure.** — The usual method of action in extradition cases, is for some police officer, or other special agent, to obtain proper papers in his own country and go with them to a foreign country, and there, with the aid of his government's representative to that country, prosecute his case and return with the fugitive in his custody to the country having jurisdiction of the crime.[11]

§ 216. **Matter of Treaty or Comity.** — Although the matter of extradition is usually governed by treaty, it is not necessarily so, for the matter in absence of a treaty rests entirely with the government on which the demand is made, and each government may surrender although no treaty exists. And where a treaty does exist, the country upon which the demand is made, may, through comity,—

[10] In re Ferez, 7 Blatchf. (U. S. C. C.) 35.
[11] 8 Op. Atty. Gen. 521.

that is, good will,— deliver up a fugitive from justice for a crime not mentioned in the existing treaty.[12]

§ 217. **No Comity on Part of United States.** — The United States, however, has always declined to surrender criminals, unless bound by treaty to do so,[13] and the courts of this country possess no power to arrest and surrender to a foreign country fugitives from justice, except as authorized by treaty stipulations and Acts of Congress passed in pursuance thereof.[14]

§ 218. **Surrendered Fugitive may be tried only for Crime upon which he was extradited.** — A fugitive surrendered by a foreign government can only be tried for the crime for which he was extradited,[15] until after he has been released from custody and given sufficient opportunity to return to the country from which he was extradited. After sufficient time for this purpose has elapsed, he may be re-arrested and tried for any offence with which he is charged.

[12] Ex parte Foss, 102 Cal. 347.
[13] Holmes *v.* Jennison, 14 Pet. (U. S.) 540.
[14] In re Kaine, 14 How. (U. S.) 103.
[15] U. S. *v.* Watts, 14 Fed. Rep. (U. S.) 130; U. S. *v.* Raucher, 119 U. S. 407; Foster *v.* Neilson, 2 Pet. (U. S.) 254; Ex parte Hibbs, 26 Fed. Rep. (U. S.) 421; State *v.* Vanderpool, 39 Ohio St. 273; Com. *v.* Hawes, 13 Bush (Ky.), 697.

§ 219. **Kidnapped Fugitive tried for any Crime.** — But where a fugitive from justice has been kidnapped from a country, between which country and the United States an extradition treaty exists, the prisoner may be tried for an offence not named in the existing treaty,[16] because the United States in the trial of the accused owes no duty to the State from which he was kidnapped, the treaty of extradition not having entered into the incident.

§ 220. **Fugitive in Rendition tried for any Crime.** — As between the different States of the United States, any fugitive given up in rendition may be tried for the offence named in the requisition, or any other offence not named therein.[17]

Where a person has been returned in rendition, as a fugitive from justice from another State, and upon trial has been acquitted of the offence charged, he may be at once re-arrested and prosecuted upon another charge, without being given an opportunity to return to the State of his previous asylum.[18]

But where one has been extradited for an offence

---

[16] Ker *v.* Illinois, 119 U. S. 436.

[17] Mahon *v.* Justice, 127 U. S. 700; Carr *v.* State, 104 Ala. 4; Com. *v.* Wright, 158 Mass. 149; State *v.* Stewart, 60 Wis. 587; Lascelles *v.* Georgia, 148 U. S. 537; Lascelles *v.* State, 90 Ga. 347; State *v.* Kealy, 89 Iowa, 94; People *v.* Cross, 135 N. Y. 536; In re Miles, 52 Vt. 609; State *v.* Glover, 112 N. C. 896. *Contra:* Ex parte McKnight, 48 Ohio St. 588; State *v.* Hall, 40 Kan. 338.

[18] Browning *v.* Abrams, 51 How. Pr. (N. Y.) 172; Reid *v.* Ham, 54 Minn. 305. *Contra:* Compton *v.* Wilder, 40 Ohio St. 130.

which is not a crime, he cannot be detained to answer for another offence until he has had an opportunity to return to the State whence he was extradited.[19] And one under bail cannot be considered as having an opportunity to return to the State whence he was taken,[20] because one under bail cannot be considered as having a right to leave the State in which he is bailed.

§ 221. **Jurisdiction procured by Stratagem.** — A prisoner cannot set up as a ground for discharge that he has been enticed into the State by fraudulent representations,[21] nor that the extradition proceedings in the other State were irregular,[22] nor that he was kidnapped and thus brought into the jurisdiction of the trial court.[23]

So where one was indicted in Kentucky for murder, and escaped to West Virginia, from which State he was forcibly abducted to Kentucky, it was held that the prisoner was not entitled to be discharged from custody under a writ of *habeas corpus* from the Circuit Court of the United States. And the fact that extradition proceedings had been instituted was not material.[24]

---

[19] In re Cannon, 47 Mich. 481. See also Ex parte Slanson, 73 Fed. Rep. (U. S.) 666.

[20] In re Cannon, supra cit.

[21] In re Brown, 4 N. Y. Cr. Rep. 576.

[22] In re Miles, 52 Vt. 609.

[23] Ker v. Illinois, 119 U. S. 436; Mahon v. Justice, 127 U. S. 700.

[24] Mahon v. Justice, supra cit.

§ 222. **Constitutional Provisions.** — Respecting interstate rendition it is provided by the Constitution of the United States, Article IV, Section 2, that "A person charged in any State with treason, felony, or other crime, who shall flee from justice and be found in another State, shall, upon demand from the executive authority of the State from which he fled, be delivered up, to be removed to the State having jurisdiction of the crime." The words "treason, felony, or other crimes" cover misdemeanors as well as felonies.[25] It is, however, safe to say that there will be no rendition for offences that are too trivial either in financial importance, or in moral obliquity, to receive the attention of the executive authority of the State in which the fugitive has taken refuge, to the exclusion of State matters of greater importance.

§ 223. **Arrest may be before Extradition Proceedings are begun.** — A fugitive from justice may be arrested in the State to which he has fled, even before the rendition proceedings have been started,[26] by making complaint upon oath before the proper magistrate, clearly setting forth the facts constituting the offence.[27]

---

[25] Ex parte Reggel, 114 U. S. 642; In re Greenough, 31 Vt. 279; Morton v. Skinner, 48 Ind. 123; Com. v. Johnston, 12 Pa. Co. Ct. 263; State v. Hudson, 2 Ohio N. P. 1.

[26] In re Fetter, 3 Zab. (N. J.) 311. But see Malcolmson v. Scott, 56 Mich. 459.

[27] In re Heyward, 1 Sandf. (N. Y.) 701.

§ 224. **Preliminary Proceedings before Requisition.** — Before there can be a requisition or rendition in such interstate matter, there must have been an indictment found, or an affidavit made before a proper magistrate, in the State from which the requisition papers issue, charging the fugitive with treason, felony, or other crime,[28] a copy of which indictment or affidavit must be certified as authentic by the Governor of the State from which the fugitive fled, and presented with the requisition papers. Upon the matter being thus properly presented, the executive of the State to which the fugitive has fled should cause the arrest and detention of the fugitive for a period of not longer than six months, until the agent of the State presenting the requisition may appear.[29]

§ 225. **Nature of Crime charged.** — As the offence charged must be a crime, rendition will not lie for a prosecution in bastardy proceedings.[30]

The term "other crime," as an extraditable offence, includes statutory as well as common law crimes;[31] in fact any offence indictable by the laws of the demanding State may furnish grounds for extradition.[32]

[28] Ex parte White, 49 Cal. 433.
[29] Act of Cong. Feb. 12, 1793; Stat. Large, 302.
[30] In re Cannon, 47 Mich. 481.
[31] People ex rel. Jourdan v. Donahue, 84 N. Y. 438.
[32] Brown's Case, 112 Mass. 409.

§ 226. **Surrender in Rendition is Obligatory.** — The duty to surrender in rendition, being commanded by the Constitution of the United States, Article IV, Section 2, is obligatory, and does not rest on comity, as in extradition.[33]

§ 227. **Who is a Fugitive from Justice?** — Under a statute providing interstate rendition, a person is a fugitive from justice when he has committed a crime within a State, and withdrawn from the jurisdiction of its courts without waiting to abide its consequences,[34] and it matters not that some other cause than a desire to flee induced such withdrawal.[35]

To warrant the extradition of such fugitive from justice, it is not necessary that he should have left the State wherein the crime was committed for the purpose of avoiding a prosecution, either anticipated or begun, but it is sufficient that having committed an offence which by the laws of the State constitutes a crime, when it comes to subject him to the process of the State to answer for his offence, he has left its jurisdiction and is found

---

[33] In re Voorhees, 32 N. J. 145.

[34] State v. Hall, 115 N. C. 811; In re Voorhees, 32 N. J. 141; Hibler v. State, 43 Tex. 197; In re White, 55 Fed. Rep. (U. S.) 54.

[35] White v. Vallely, 14 U. S. App. 87; In re Block, 87 Fed. Rep. (U. S.) 981; Roberts v. Reilly, 116 U. S. 80; In re Sultan, 115 N. C. 57; State v. Richter, 37 Minn. 436; In re White, 55 Fed. Rep. (U. S.) 54.

within the territory of another State.[36] Extradition does not lie for a party who is not a fugitive from justice although he has constructively committed a crime in a State.[37]

[36] White *v.* Vallely, 14 U. S. App. 87.
[37] Wilcox *v.* Nolze, 34 Ohio St. 520; Mohr's Case, 73 Ala. 503.

CHAPTER XI

EVIDENCE NECESSARY TO ESTABLISH THE OFFENCE

§ 228. **Proof must be Beyond a Reasonable Doubt.** — An officer who, upon his own responsibility, makes an arrest without a warrant, is generally called upon to show that an offence was committed which justified him in arresting the offender.

To establish the crime he has the burden of proving, beyond a reasonable doubt, all the elements which go to make up the offence.[1] And the mere preponderance of evidence is never sufficient to convict one of crime, but a greater degree of proof is necessary, — proof that will not allow a reasonable doubt of the prisoner's guilt to remain in the mind of the court, or of the jury, as the case may be.[2]

§ 229. **Burden of Proof Remains on Prosecutor.** — And this burden remains with him to the end of the case, for the burden of proof as to the necessity of establishing the ultimate fact to be proved, that is, the fact of the commission of the crime, or the

---

[1] Farley *v.* State, 127 Ind. 419; State *v.* Rogers, 119 N. C. 793.

[2] Lee *v.* State, 76 Ga. 498; Gray *v.* Com., 101 Pa. 380.

corpus delicti,[3] the identity of the prisoner,[4] and the guilt of the accused never shifts from the prosecution.[5]

§ 230. **Burden of Giving Evidence may shift.**— While the burden of proof in making out a *prima facie* case, where a crime is charged, never shifts from the prosecution, yet where the defendant, instead of producing proof to negative the proof adduced by the prosecution, proposes to show another and distinct proposition which avoids the effect of the evidence adduced by the prosecution, there the burden of proof, or rather the burden of giving evidence, does shift, and rests upon the party who proposes to show the latter fact.[6] As where the prisoner endeavors to prove an *alibi*, that being a new and distinct proposition which, if proved,

---

[3] Rex *v.* Burdette, 4 B. & Ald. (Eng. K. B.) 95; State *v.* Davidson, 30 Vt. 377; People *v.* Palmer, 109 N. Y. 110; Willard *v.* State, 27 Tex. App. 386. The corpus delicti cannot be established alone by confessions of the accused; other evidence is necessary. People *v.* Hennessey, 15 Wend. (N. Y.) 147; Gore *v.* People, 162 Ill. 265; State *v.* German, 54 Mo. 526; People *v.* Tarbox, 115 Cal. 57; Attaway *v.* State, 35 Tex. Cr. 403; Holland *v.* State, 39 Fla. 178; Harden *v.* State, 109 Ala. 50.

[4] Winslow *v.* State, 76 Ala. 42; Gore *v.* People, 162 Ill. 265.

[5] People *v.* Plath, 100 N. Y. 590; Jones *v.* State, 51 Ohio St. 331; Williams *v.* People, 101 Ill. 385; State *v.* Harvey, 131 Mo. 339; Gravely *v.* State, 38 Neb. 871.

[6] Powers *v.* Russell, 13 Pick. (Mass.) 69.

will avoid the effect of the plaintiff's evidence, the burden of proving the *alibi* rests upon the accused.[7]

§ 231. **Burden of Proof does not shift.** — Yet even there the burden of proof does not shift in a practical sense, for if the prisoner fails to establish the new and distinct proposition which he interposes in his own defence, and which need only be established by a preponderance of evidence, whatever evidence he does produce to that end must be weighed in the balance, and if upon all evidence produced by both parties, there remains a reasonable doubt of the prisoner's guilt, he must be acquitted,[8] for the prisoner is always entitled to the benefit of a reasonable doubt.

§ 232. **Presumption of Innocence.** — While it is a well-established principle of law that "a man is presumed to be innocent until he is found guilty," this presumption has no other effect than casting upon the State the burden of proving the guilt of the accused beyond a reasonable doubt. It has no weight as evidence in the trial, and although it calls for evidence from the State it is not evidence for the accused.[9]

---

[7] Com. v. Choate, 105 Mass. 451; Carlton v. People, 150 Ill. 181; State v. Taylor, 118 Mo. 153; Towns v. State, 111 Ala. 1; People v. Pichette, 111 Mich. 461.

[8] Com. v. Choate, 105 Mass. 452; Walters v. State, 39 Ohio St. 215; State v. Chee Gong, 16 Oreg. 534; Borrego v. Ter., 8 N. M. 446.

[9] State v. Smith, 65 Conn. 285.

EVIDENCE TO ESTABLISH THE OFFENCE   135

The accused starts into a trial with the presumption of innocence in his favor, and it stays with him until it is driven out of the case by testimony. And whenever the evidence shows beyond a reasonable doubt that the crime as charged has been committed, or that a crime exists, then the presumption of innocence disappears from the case.[10]

§ 233. **Burden when Charge is Use of Excessive Force.** — Where an officer is on trial charged with using excessive force in the act of making an arrest, the burden is on the State to show the use of extreme measures. And all the circumstances surrounding the act of arrest should be looked into to determine that question.[11]

§ 234. **Burden to show Offence in Officer's Presence.** — Where an officer arrests a person without a warrant, for an offence less than a felony, the burden is on him, when sued in trespass therefor, to show that the offence was in fact committed in his presence.[12]

§ 235. **Burden to show Authority to arrest.** — And a person who assumes to arrest another who, when sued in trespass therefor, attempts to justify his act on the ground that he acted as a police offi-

---

[10] Allen v. U. S., 164 U. S. 500. *Contra:* Farley v. State, 127 Ind. 421.

[11] State v. Dierberger, 96 Mo. 666.

[12] Shanley v. Wells, 71 Ill. 78.

cer, must not merely show that he was an officer *de facto*, but that he was an officer *de jure,* that he was legally and duly qualified to act as an officer.[13]

§ 236. **Burden to show License.** — In an action for selling articles without a license, the burden is upon the defendant to show that he has complied with the law and has a license to sell.[14] But the presumption of innocence is still with the defendant.[15]

§ 237. **Weight of Evidence on Insanity.** — Respecting the weight of evidence necessary to establish the insanity of the defendant in a criminal case, there are two distinct lines of authority. The weight of authority in this matter seems to be that the defendant in a criminal action has the burden of establishing his plea of insanity only to such an extent as to create a reasonable doubt of his sanity.[16] The other view is that the defendant must establish his insanity by a greater degree of evidence, — that which is a preponderance of the testimony.[17]

[13] Short *v.* Symmes, 150 Mass. 298.

[14] Com. *v.* Holstine, 132 Pa. St. 357; Williams *v.* People, 121 Ill. 84; Com. *v.* Thurlow, 24 Pick. (Mass) 374; Liggitt *v.* People, 26 Col. 364; State *v.* Sorrell, 98 N. C. 738; State *v.* Keggon, 55 N. H. 19; State *v.* Shelton, 16 Wash. 590; People *v.* Curtis, 95 Mich. 212; Birr *v.* People, 113 Ill. 647.

[15] Com. *v.* Holstine, supra cit.

[16] Davis *v.* U. S., 160 U. S. 469.

[17] People *v.* Bemmerly, 98 Cal. 299; Loegrove *v.* State, 31 Tex. Cr. Rep. 491.

§ 238. **Evidence of Bad Character.** — Bad character is not admissible to show a disposition to do a particular thing, but may sometimes be offered to throw light on a motive.[18]

When character is not itself in issue, evidence of bad character can never be introduced by the prosecution until the prisoner has opened the way by producing evidence of his own good character.[19] So the fact that the defendant was an ex-convict, having been imprisoned before, was not competent evidence against him, he not having introduced evidence in support of his good character.[20] But if the accused takes the stand in his own behalf, his reputation for veracity may be attacked just the same as that of any other witness.[21]

§ 239. **Character Evidence must be General.** — Evidence as to character must be confined to general reputation, and must not touch upon particular acts.[22] And, as a general rule, evidence as to char-

---

[18] People v. McLaughlin, 150 N. Y. 365; Wright v. State, 108 Ala. 60.

[19] State v. Lapage, 57 N. H. 245; People v. White, 14 Wend. (N. Y.) 111; People v. Fair, 43 Cal. 137; State v. Hull, 18 R. I. 207; Young v. Com., 6 Bush (Ky.), 312; State v. Creson, 38 Mo. 372; Reg. v. Rowton, 10 Cox C. C. (Eng.) 25.

[20] People v. White, supra cit.

[21] Com. v. O'Brien, 119 Mass. 342.

[22] Com. v. O'Brien, supra cit.; Com. v. Harris, 131 Mass. 336; Stalcup v. State, 146 Ind. 270; State v. McGee, 81 Iowa, 17; Evans v. State, 109 Ala. 11; Garner v. State, 28

acter, when admissible in criminal cases, is to be confined to the particular trait in question.[23]

§ 240. **Good Character is always Admissible.** — Good character may be shown by the prisoner to establish the improbability of his having committed the crime with which he is charged, and it may be such strong evidence as to create a reasonable doubt in the face of overwhelming facts of guilt.[24]

§ 241. **Nature of Character Evidence.** — Evidence to prove character may be by the testimony of those who know the character of the party, or by the reputation which the party bears in the community, or by particular conduct. And as the character of a man is subject to a change, it is very material that character evidence relate to the time near when the crime charged was committed.

§ 242. **Conduct as Evidence of Guilt.** — It is competent evidence against the prisoner that he

Fla. 113; Basye v. State, 45 Neb. 261; State v. Lapage, 57 N. H. 245; Hirschman v. People, 101 Ill. 574.

[23] Clark v. Brown, 116 Mass. 504.

[24] People v. Van Dam, 107 Mich. 425; Com. v. Wilson, 152 Mass. 12; Com. v. Leonard, 140 Mass. 473; Aneals v. People, 134 Ill. 401; Hall v. State, 132 Ind. 317; Stewart v. State, 22 Ohio St. 477; State v. Schleagel, 50 Kan. 325; State v. Donohoo, 22 W. Va. 761; Parrish v. Com , 81 Va. 1; State v. Ward, 73 Iowa, 532; Gibson v. State, 89 Ala. 121; Hardtke v. State, 67 Wis. 552; Edgington v. U. S., 164 U. S. 361.

was silent when charged with the crime,[25] or that he destroyed evidence of his guilt,[26] or marks of ownership,[27] or that he took to flight,[28] concealment, or disguise,[29] or attempted to stifle investigation, or possessed the fruits of his crime,[30] or that there are unexplained suspicious appearances, or that he attempted to commit the same crime at another time, or that he used communicated threats.[31]

§ 242 a. **Possession of Stolen Goods as Evidence.** — When a theft has been committed, and, immediately after the commission of the crime, the stolen property is found in possession of the party sus-

[25] Rex v. Smithies, 5 C. & P. (Eng. N. P.) 332; Ackerson v. People, 124 Ill. 572; People v. McCrea, 32 Cal. 98; Franklin v. State, 69 Ga. 36. *Contra:* Com. v. McDermott, 123 Mass. 440; Com. v. Walker, 13 Allen (Mass.), 570; Com. v. Kenney, 12 Metc. (Mass.) 235.

[26] So. P. R. Co. v. Johnson, 44 U. S. App. 1.

[27] Wilson v. U. S., 162 U. S. 613.

[28] State v. Frederic, 69 Me. 400; State v. Rodman, 62 Iowa, 456; Bell v. State, 115 Ala. 25; Sewell v. State, 76 Ga. 836.

[29] Com. v. McMahon, 145 Pa. St. 413; State v. Bradneck, 69 Conn. 212; Com. v. Brigham, 147 Mass. 414.

[30] Goon Bow v. People, 160 Ill. 438; Wilson v. U. S., supra cit.

[31] Ward v. State, 30 Tex. App. 687; Ford v. State, 112 Ind. 373; People v. Duck, 61 Cal. 387; Painter v. People, 147 Ill. 462; Griffin v. State, 90 Ala. 596; Linehan v. State, 113 Ala. 70; Brooks v. Com., 100 Ky. 194; State v. Edwards, 34 La. 1012; State v. McKinney, 31 Kan. 570.

pected of the theft, it is *prima facie* evidence of the guilt of the person in whose possession the property is found, and unless other circumstances surrounding the case serve to create a reasonable doubt, is sufficient to convict.[32]

And if the finding of the property in the possession of the accused is *immediately* after the commission of the offence, it is almost conclusive evidence of his guilt; but the presumption of guilt weakens as time elapses.[33]

Although the unexplained possession of property may sometimes justify an arrest on suspicion, the defendant is never bound at his trial to explain the possession of recently stolen property, because the burden of proving the offence beyond a reasonable doubt is on the prosecution.[34]

§ 243. **Intoxication as a Defence where Specific Intent is Essential.** — Voluntary intoxication is no defence to a criminal charge.[35] But where a specific

---

[32] Com. v. Randall, 119 Mass. 107; Keating v. People, 160 Ill. 486; State v. Walker, 41 Iowa, 217; Gablick v. People, 40 Mich. 292.

[33] Gablick v. People, 40 Mich. 292; Com. v. Montgomery, 11 Metc. (Mass.) 534; White v. State, 72 Ala. 195; Belote v. State, 36 Miss. 96.

[34] Hoge v. People, 117 Ill. 44; State v. Miner, 107 Iowa, 656; Van Straaten v. People, 26 Col. 184; Heed v. State, 25 Wis. 421; Smith v. State, 58 Ind. 340.

[35] 4 Bl. Com. 26; 1 Hale's P. C. 32; Hopt v. Utah, 104 U. S. 631; State v. Tatro, 50 Vt. 483; Crosby v. People, 137 Ill. 341; Shannahan v. Com., 8 Bush (Ky.), 463; State

intent, that is, an intent to do a certain thing, is a necessary ingredient of the crime charged, intoxication may be set up in defence to show that the specific intent could not exist.[36]

For example, a breaking and entering of a dwelling-house in the night-time will not constitute burglary unless at the time of the breaking and entering there exists a specific intent to commit a felony therein, and the intoxication may be of such a degree as to negative the existence of this specific intent.

§ 244. **Confession by Intoxicated Person.** — A confession made by a party who is so intoxicated as not to understand it, is not admissible.[37]

§ 245. **Confession, if not Voluntary, is Inadmissible.** — A confession of the prisoner is not admissible as evidence unless it was voluntarily made, and was

v. West, 157 Mo. 309; Conley v. Com., 98 Ky. 125; People v. Miller, 114 Cal. 10; Colee v. State, 75 Ind. 511; Rex v. Carroll, 7 C. & P. (Eng. N. P.) 145.

[36] Rex v. Pitman, 2 C. & P. (Eng. N. P.) 423; Com. v. Hagenlock, 140 Mass. 125; Crosby v. People, 137 Ill. 342; Schwabacher v. People, 165 Ill. 629; Com. v. Dorsey, 103 Mass. 412; State v. Garvey, 11 Minn. 154; Warner v. State, 56 N. J. L. 686; Lancaster v. State, 2 Lea (Tenn.), 575; State v. Fiske, 63 Conn. 388; Jenkins v. State, 93 Ga. 1; Pigman v. State, 14 Ohio, 555; Cline v. State, 43 Ohio St. 332; Hopt v. Utah, 104 U. S. 631; People v. Walker, 38 Mich. 156; Englehardt v. State, 88 Ala. 100; People v. Young, 102 Cal. 411.

[37] Com. v. Howe, 9 Gray (Mass.), 110.

not inspired by influence of hope or fear.[38] And the burden as to voluntary character of the confession is on the prosecution.[39] If the confession was obtained by any promises, or threats, of some one in authority over the accused, it is not admissible.

So where a police officer arrested the defendant for larceny from the person, he said to him: " If you will get the money it will not be used as evidence against you; I want to get back the money." On the next day the defendant confessed to another police officer. It was held that, although the statements of the second officer were admissible, the refusal of the judge at the trial for the offence to instruct the jury that they ought to give no weight to the confession, if they thought it was made under the influence of the inducements, gave the defendant a good ground of exception.[40]

If an officer should say to the accused, " You had better tell the truth," or, " You had better tell about it," any confession given by the accused thereafter would be incompetent; because such language would naturally convey to the mind of the accused that he would gain some advantage if he confessed his guilt. On the other hand, if the officer merely asked the prisoner to tell the truth, this

---

[38] Com. v. Culver, 126 Mass. 464; Com. v. Burroughs, 162 Mass. 513.

[39] Hopt v. Utah, 110 U. S. 587; Roesel v. State, 62 N. J. 216

[40] Com. v. Cullen, 111 Mass. 435.

would not imply that the officer promised any advantage if he confessed, and a confession resultant therefrom would be admissible.[41]

And a confession procured by artifice, deception, or falsehood, if otherwise competent, is admissible.[42]

To exclude the confession, the promise of favor must have been made by one in authority,[43] and respecting punishment for the crime charged;[44] and the promise must have been relied on in making the confession.

§ 246. **Entire Confession must go in.** — When a confession is introduced as evidence, the entire confession must go in,[45] and it is always open to explanation by the accused,[46] for the doctrine of estoppel does not apply in criminal cases.[47]

§ 247. **Collateral Evidence obtained by Confession is Admissible.** — Although a confession obtained by improper means is not admissible against the

---

[41] Com. v. Preece, 140 Mass. 276; Flagg v. People, 40 Mich. 706; Robinson v. People, 159 Ill. 119; State v. Day, 55 Vt. 570. *Contra:* State v. Bradford, 156 Mo. 91; State v. Komstell, 61 Pac. Rep. (Kan.) 805.

[42] Burton v. State, 107 Ala. 108; State v. Phelps, 74 Mo. 136; Andrews v. People, 117 Ill. 201; People v. Barker, 60 Mich. 277; Osborn v. Com., 14 Ky. L. 246; Heldt v. State, 20 Neb. 492.

[43] Com. v. Knapp, 10 Pick. (Mass.) 477.

[44] State v. Tatro, 50 Vt. 483.

[45] People v. Gelabert, 39 Cal. 663.

[46] State v. Brown, 1 Mo. App. 86.

[47] State v. Hutchinson, 60 Iowa, 478.

accused, yet any collateral evidence obtained by means of the confession may be used against the prisoner.[48] As where, by promise of favor, a confession was obtained which disclosed the stolen property located in the bed of the prisoner, the confession was inadmissible, but the fact that the property was found in the possession of the prisoner is admissible.[49]

§ 248. **Criminal Act and Criminal Intent must be Concurrent.** — To constitute a crime, it is necessary that there exist in the mind of the accused a criminal intent at the very time when he does the criminal act, — that is, the act and the intent must co-exist.

§ 249. **Criminal Capacity of Children.** — The law conclusively presumes that a child under the age of seven years cannot entertain a criminal intent, and therefore can never be guilty of a crime.[50] A child between the ages of seven and fourteen years is only *prima facie* incapable of committing a crime, that is, the presumption that the child has not the criminal capacity may be rebutted by proof that

---

[48] Com. v. Knapp, 9 Pick. (Mass.) 496; Williams v. Com., 27 Gratt. (Va.) 997; Gates v. People, 14 Ill. 437; White v. State, 3 Heisk. (Tenn.) 338; Duffy v. People, 26 N. Y. 588; People v. Barker, 60 Mich. 277.

[49] Rex v. Warickshall, 1 Leach C. C. (4th ed.) 263; State v. Graham, 74 N. C. 646.

[50] People v. Townsend, 3 Hill (N. Y.), 479; 4 Bl. Com. 23; 1 Hale's P. C. 27.

he is capable of forming the necessary criminal intent.[51] In case of a crime charged against one under fourteen years of age, the burden of proof is on the prosecution to show that the party so charged has the capacity of forming a criminal intent, that is, of entertaining a guilty knowledge that he was doing wrong.[52]

§ 250. **Dying Declarations.** — A statement made by one who believes himself to be in a dying condition, by reason of the solemnity of the occasion and the disposition of the injured party to speak the truth at that time,[53] is very weighty evidence concerning the inflicting of the wound which caused the homicide, or the circumstances connected therewith.[54] Such statements are called "dying declarations," and may be either oral or written, or even by signs.[55]

[51] Com. v. Mead, 10 Allen (Mass.), 398; Angelo v. People, 96 Ill. 209; State v. Tice, 90 Mo. 112; State v. Adams, 76 Mo. 355; State v. Fowler, 52 Iowa, 103; Godfrey v. State, 31 Ala. 323; State v. Aaron, 4 N. J. L. 231.

[52] Reg. v. Smith, 1 Cox C. C. (Eng.) 260.

[53] Rex v. Drummond, 1 Leach C. C. (4th ed.) 337; People v. Olmstead, 30 Mich. 431.

[54] Scott v. People, 63 Ill. 508; Wroe v. State, 20 Ohio St. 460; State v. Garrand, 5 Oreg. 216; State v. Shelton, 47 N. C. 364; Savage v. State, 18 Fla. 909; State v. Reed, 137 Mo. 125; State v. Pearce, 56 Minn. 226; Starr v. Com., 97 Ky. 193; People v. Davis, 56 N. Y. 103; Sullivan v. State, 102 Ala. 135; Bryant v. State, 80 Ga. 272; Ex parte Fatheree, 34 Tex. Cr. 594; Puryear v. Com., 83 Va. 51.

[55] Com. v. Casey, 11 Cush. (Mass.) 417; Mockabee v.

§ 251. **Condition of the Declarant.** — The party making such declaration must be in apprehension of immediate death, and without hope of recovery,[56] and death must eventually occur, although the fact that the death does not occur as soon as expected, will not render the declaration inadmissible.[57]

§ 252. **Competency of the Declarant.** — The declaration must have been made by one who, if living, would be a competent witness in court.[58] So the dying declaration of a child four years of age was held to be incompetent.[59]

§ 253. **Best Evidence Only is Competent.** — Whenever evidence to establish a crime is given,

---

Com., 78 Ky. 382; Daughdrill v. State, 113 Ala. 7; State v. Somnier, 33 La. 239.

[56] Com. v. Roberts, 108 Mass. 296; Com. v Bishop, 165 Mass. 148; Simons v. People, 150 Ill. 73; State v. Wilson, 121 Mo. 434; Archibald v. State, 122 Ind. 122; Vaughan v. Com., 86 Ky. 431; State v. Baldwin, 79 Iowa, 714; State v. Daniel, 31 La. 91; Com. v. Mika, 171 Pa. St. 273; Cole v. State, 105 Ala. 76; Whittaker v. State, 79 Ga. 87.

[57] Com. v. Haney, 127 Mass. 455; State v. Reed, 53 Kan. 767; People v. Weaver, 108 Mich. 649; State v. Craine, 120 N. C. 601; People v. Chase, 79 Hun (N. Y.), 296; Moore v. State, 96 Tenn. 209; White v. State, 111 Ala. 92; Evans v. State, 58 Ark. 47; Radford v. State, 33 Tex. Cr. 520.

[58] Rex v. Pike, 3 C. & P. (Eng N. P.) 598; State v. Ah Lee, 8 Oreg. 214; Rex v. Drummond, 1 Leach C. C. (Eng.) 4th ed. 337; State v. Elliott, 45 Iowa, 486; People v. Sanford, 43 Cal. 29.

[59] Rex v. Pike, supra cit.

it must be the best evidence obtainable, and any evidence which presupposes better evidence will be rejected. Therefore one may not ordinarily testify to what another person has said, because the party originally making the statement was not under oath or subject to a cross-examination.

And then, too, it would be better evidence if from the lips of the person who made the original statement, for the party who heard the statement might not have correctly understood it But the sole reason for the rejection of such testimony is that the party was not under oath or open to cross-examination.

§ 254. **Doubt Always goes to Benefit of Accused.** — In all cases of doubt arising in the criminal law, the benefit of the doubt should be given to the accused,[60] and that too whether the doubt arises upon a construction of the law applicable to the case, or upon the evidence of the guilt of the prisoner.

§ 255. **Ignorance of Law.** — It is a maxim of the law that "Ignorance of the law excuses no one."[61] There seems, however, to be one exception to that rule, in that where a person takes property under such circumstances that it amounts to larceny, he is not guilty of larceny if he took it under a *bona*

---

[60] O'Neil v. State, 48 Ga. 66.
[61] Thompson v. State, 26 Tex. App. 94; U. S. v. Anthony, 11 Blatchf. (U. S.) 200.

fide belief that it was his own, even though the mistake was one of the law governing ownership.[62]

So where A. had set snares on the land of B., and a servant of B., finding the snares with an entrapped pheasant in one of them, appropriated them under authority of a statute, to the use of his master. A., finding the servant had appropriated the snares and pheasant, forcibly compelled the servant to give them up, under the belief that they remained his property. *Held*, no robbery, because his *bona fide* impression that he was only getting his own property showed that the *animus furandi*, — the intent to steal, necessary to a robbery, was not present.[63]

And where the defendant lent the father of the plaintiff two hundred dollars, and took his note therefor, payable on demand, with interest, and the father died, leaving the note unpaid, the son appropriated all the property of his deceased father to his own use, taking out no letters of administration. Subsequently while the son was counting money in the presence of the defendant, the defendant seized the money, saying, " that she had a right to it; that she had been looking for it for a long time, and now she had got it; that the old man owed her, and now it was time for her to get her own." *Held*, that

---

[62] Com. *v.* Stebbins, 8 Gray (Mass.), 495; Com. *v.* Doane, 1 Cush. (Mass.) 5; State *v.* Holmes, 17 Mo. 379; Dye *v.* Com., 7 Gratt. (Va.) 662; People *v.* Husband, 36 Mich. 306; Rex *v.* Hall, 3 C. & P. (Eng. N. P.) 409.

[63] Rex *v.* Hall, supra cit.

the instruction to the jury, that the defendant was not guilty of larceny if she took the money under an honest belief that she had a legal right to take it, was clearly correct.[64]

[64] Com. *v.* Stebbins, 8 Gray (Mass.) 495.

CHAPTER XII

EXEMPTION FROM ARREST

§ 256. Sovereigns and Diplomatic Agents. — The law of nations protects the sovereign of a friendly foreign country and his retinue of servants from arrest while passing through or sojourning temporarily in our country.[1] The law also protects his ambassador or other diplomatic agent sent by him to this country,[2] and this protection is not extended to the person alone of such functionary, but to his secretary, attendants, and retinue, his couriers and domestic servants as well.[3] Neither he nor his

---

[1] Wheaton's Int. Law, 6th ed. 143, 146.

[2] Dupont v. Pichon, 4 Dall. (U. S.) 321; Woolsey Int. Law, 135. The remedy against a diplomatic agent who transgresses the criminal laws so as to affect individuals only, is to demand his recall, and if the demand be refused, to expel him from the country. If, however, the crime affect the safety of the government, the government may, if necessary to its safety, seize and hold him until the danger be passed, or forcibly expel him from the country. 7 Op. Atty -Gen. (U. S.) 367.

[3] U. S. v. Lafontaine, 4 Cranch (U. S. C. C.), 173; Lockwood v. Coysgarne, 3 Burr. (Eng. K. B.) 1676; Inglis v. Sailors Snug Harbor, 3 Pet. (U. S) 99; Respublica v. De Longchamps, 1 Dall. (Pa.) 111. Although the secretary of a minister is included, the wife of the secretary is not exempt. English v. Caballero, 3 D. & R. (Eng. K. B.) 25.

are subject to the civil or criminal processes of our courts.

A foreign minister cannot waive his privilege, because it is that of his sovereign; and an attache of a foreign legation is a "minister."[4] The fact that the officer did not know him to be such is no excuse for the arrest.[5]

But this immunity from arrest does not prevent a citizen of our country from exercising the usual rights of self-defence when attacked by such exempted person.[6]

§ 257. **Commercial Agents. — Consuls.** — Consul-generals are exempt,[7] but consuls are not,[8] they being mere commercial agents, owing a temporary allegiance to the State, and not diplomatic agents, who owe no allegiance to the State.

§ 258. **Attorneys at Law.** — Among others who are exempt from civil arrest only, are attorneys at law while attending court.[9] But the privilege of

[4] U. S. v. Benner, Baldwin (U. S. C. C.), 234.
[5] Ibid. But see Chase v. Fish, 16 Me. 132.
[6] U. S. v. Ortiga, 4 Wash. (U. S. C. C.) 531.
[7] Marshall v. Critico, 9 East (Eng. K. B.), 447. *Contra:* Com. v. Kosloff, 5 S. & R. (Pa.) 545.
[8] Com. v. Kosloff, supra cit.
[9] Secor v. Bell, 18 Johns. (N. Y.) 52. In Georgia it is held that this rule of the common law never obtained in America, owing to the essential difference in the relations which the profession sustains both to the courts and the public in England and this country. Elam v. Lewis, 19 Ga. 608.

attorneys is not so much for their benefit as it is for the benefit of their clients,[10] and is therefore confined to attorneys who practice.[11]

§ 259. **Other Exemptions.** — So also are bail exempt while attending court as such;[12] a petitioning bankrupt attending before commissioners to be examined;[13] insolvent debtors lawfully discharged,[14] — but not when sued on subsequent liabilities or promises;[15] clergymen while performing divine service, or going to or returning from the performance of such service on any day of the week;[16] militia men on military duty,[17] except commissioned officers under certain circumstances;[18] electors while attending, or going to or returning from a public election;[19] jurors attending court;[20] sheriffs and

[10] Gardner v. Jessop, 2 Wils. (Eng. C. P.) 44; Mayor of Norwich v. Berry, 4 Burr. (Eng. K. B.) 2113; Wiltshire v. Lloyd, 3 Doug. (Eng. K. B.) 381.

[11] Goldsmith v. Baynard, 2 Wils. (Eng. C. P.) 232; Mayor of Norwich v. Berry, supra cit.

[12] Rimmer v. Green, 1 Maule & S. (Eng. K. B.) 638.

[13] In re Kimball, 2 Ben. (U. S.) 38.

[14] Wilmarth v. Burt, 7 Metc. (Mass.) 257; Rev. Laws of Mass. c. 163, § 95.

[15] Horton v. Moggridge, 6 Taunt. (Eng. C. P.) 563; Glazier v. Stafford, 4 Harr. (Del.) 240.

[16] Bacon's Abr. (Trespass).

[17] People v. Campbell, 40 N. Y. 133; In re Turner, 119 Fed. Rep. (U. S.) 231; Rev. Laws of Mass. c. 16, § 174.

[18] Ex parte Harlan, 39 Ala. 563.

[19] Swift v. Chamberlain, 3 Conn. 537.

[20] Ex parte McNeil, 3 Mass. 288.

other peace officers while actually engaged in the performance of their duties,[21] but not at other times,[22] except by statute.[23]

§ 260. **Government Employees.** — An employee of the United States government is not exempt from arrest on process issued by a State court on a charge of felony.[24]

And the driver of a wagon in which the mail is being carried is not exempt from arrest for driving through a crowded street at a dangerous rate of speed, by the Act of Congress prohibiting the stoppage of the mails.[25]

§ 261. **Legislators.** — Members of Congress, and State legislators, while attending their respective assemblies, or going to or returning from the same, are protected from arrest on all charges except treason, felony or " breach of the peace," which latter term includes all indictable offences.[26]

This protection to members of Congress, is given by the Constitution of the United States,[27] and that of the members of the State legislatures is gener-

[21] Welby v. Beard, Taylor (Up. Can.), 415.
[22] Coxson v. Doland, 2 Daly (N. Y.), 66.
[23] " A sheriff shall not be arrested upon mesne process, or execution in a civil action." Rev. Laws of Mass. c. 23, § 10.
[24] U. S. v. Kirby, 74 U. S. 482.
[25] U. S. v. Hart, Peters (U. S. C. C.), 390.
[26] Rawlins v. Ellis, 16 Mees. & W. (Eng. Exch.) 172.
[27] Const. U. S. Art. 1, § 6.

ally secured to them by the constitutions of the various States,[28] or by the common law. A member of a house of representatives who has been expelled by that body is no longer entitled to the protection;[29] nor is one entitled to protection who has merely been elected, but who has not yet taken his seat.[30]

§ 262. **Exemption may not always be Waived.** — Exemption from arrest is usually a personal privilege[31] which may be waived by the privileged person.[32] The privilege of a legislator, however, is not his personal privilege, but is that of the people whose representative he is, therefore the privilege cannot be waived by him.[33]

By the same line of reasoning, an attorney could not waive his privilege, for the privilege is really that of his client, whose interests would be imperiled.

§ 263. **Writ of Protection.** — A writ of protection is only *prima facie* proof of exemption from

---

[28] Hiss v. Bartlett, 3 Gray (Mass.), 468. "No member of the house of representatives shall be arrested or held to bail on mesne process, during his going unto, returning from, or his attending the general assembly." Const. Mass. c. 1, § 3, Art. 10.

[29] Hiss v. Bartlett, supra cit.

[30] Chase v. Fish, 16 Me. 132.

[31] Smith v. Jones, 76 Me. 138.

[32] Brown v. Getchell, 11 Mass. 11.

[33] Anderson v. Roundtree, 1 Pinn. (Wis.) 115. But see Chase v. Fish, supra cit.

arrest, and is of itself no further useful than as it serves to give notice to the officer about to make the arrest.[34]

§ 264. **Parties attending Court.** — This writ is not necessary to one whose duty brings him to court, in order that he may be shielded from arrest in a civil case. If a juror or any other person whose duty brings him to court, whether as a party or as a witness, is arrested while attending the court, or in going to or returning from the court, the court will, upon motion, take order for his discharge.[35] Such arrest is a contempt of court,[36] and may subject the party making the arrest to a prosecution for the offence. But this protection does not extend to one who comes to court, in his own State, as a volunteer, without summons.[37] A voluntary witness, however, from another State is protected,[38] although no witness in attendance at court is privileged from arrest when charged with an indictable offence.[39]

[34] Ex parte Daniel McNeil, 6 Mass. 264.
[35] The case of Archibald McNeil, 3 Mass. 287; Ex parte Archibald McNeil, 6 Mass. 245; Wood v. Neale, 5 Gray (Mass.), 538; Thompson's Case, 122 Mass. 428.
[36] Blight v. Fisher, Pet. C. C. (U. S.) 41; Wood v. Neale, 5 Gray (Mass.), 538; State v. Buck, 62 N. H. 670.
[37] Ex parte Daniel McNeil, supra cit.
[38] May v. Shumway, 16 Gray (Mass.), 86.
[39] Ex parte Levi, 28 Fed. Rep. (U. S.) 651.

§ 265. **Waiver of Privilege by Parties attending Court.** — The immunity from arrest, enjoyed by one who is attending court as a party to a proceeding then pending, being a personal privilege, may be waived, as by submission to arrest; and the arrested party cannot afterward object to the imprisonment as for that reason unlawful.[40] But a witness from another State, arrested before he has completely given his testimony, does not waive his privilege of exemption from arrest by giving bail.[41]

§ 266. **Persons under Guardianship.** — A spendthrift, under guardianship, is exempt from arrest on execution issued for debt or damages in a civil action, whenever the statute requires an affidavit to be made that the party sought to be arrested has been guilty of one of the fraudulent or wasteful acts specified in the statute,[42] because the property of the debtor is not under his own control, but under that of his guardian, consequently he could not be guilty of fraud in not applying it to the debt, and he may be discharged on *habeas corpus*.

Where no affidavit is required by the statute to warrant an arrest on an execution, it has been held that a lunatic under guardianship might be so arrested.[43]

---

[40] Brown *v.* Getchell, 11 Mass. 11.
[41] Dickinson *v.* Farwell, 71 N. H. 213.
[42] Blake's Case, 106 Mass. 501.
[43] Ex parte Leighton, 14 Mass. 207.

§ 267. **Officer not liable for arresting Exempted Party.** — An officer who acts according to his precept in making an arrest, is not a trespasser, although the party arrested is privileged from arrest.[44]

§ 268. **Exemption may include Going to and Coming from a Certain Place.** — The exemption from arrest in consideration of a certain character and specified place, includes the stay, and a reasonable time for going and returning,[45] but does not include delays or deviations.[46] So where a party exempted from arrest by reason of attendance at court, went out of a direct route on his return home, for the purpose of attending the funeral of his son, it was held that his privilege was forfeited by the deviation.[47] But where a voter at a public election had given in his vote, and retired to a house in the neighborhood to await the result of the official count of the votes, it was held that he was attending to the business of the election, and therefore exempt from arrest on civil process.[48] If an elector has not actually proceeded on his way to the voting-place, but is merely preparing to go, he cannot claim the privilege.[49]

A person who was alleged to have been elected to

[44] Chase *v.* Fish, 16 Me. 132.
[45] Smythe *v.* Banks, 4 Dall. (U. S.) 329.
[46] Chaffee *v.* Jones, 19 Pick. (Mass.) 260.
[47] Ibid.
[48] Swift *v.* Chamberlain, 3 Conn. 537.
[49] Hobbs *v.* Getchell, 8 Me. 187.

Congress, having been denied a seat by that body, is privileged from arrest until he reaches his home, and any delay by reason of sickness or want of funds does not remove the privilege.[50]

§ 269. **Debtors from Another State.** — Under a statute authorizing the arrest of a debtor on the ground that he is about to leave the State to avoid the payment of his debts, some courts hold that it is only a citizen of the State in which the arrest is made, and in which the debt exists, that is subject to arrest,[51] and that a citizen of another State is exempt from such arrest; while other courts hold that the statute extends to a debtor who is a citizen of another State, but who is temporarily within the State where he owes the debt, returning or intending to return home, as well.[52]

§ 270. **Statutory Exemptions.** — Exemptions from arrest, other than those hereinbefore specified, such as women, mariners, and others in certain cases, are sometimes made by statute.[53]

---

[50] Dunton v. Halstead, 2 Pa. L. J. Rep. 450.

[51] Stevenson v. Smith, 28 N. H. 12; McKay v. Ray, 63 N. C. 46.

[52] Tallemon v. Cardenas, 14 La. Ann. 509; Rutland Bank v. Barker, 27 Vt. 293.

[53] "No woman shall be arrested on mesne process, except for tort. No person shall be arrested on mesne process in a civil action for slander or libel." Rev. Laws of Mass. c. 168, § 3. See Foss v. Hildreth, 10 Allen (Mass.), 76, holding that a threat to make an arrest for slander is, under the stat-

EXEMPTION FROM ARREST 159

When a statute names a sheriff only, as exempt from arrest under civil process, the protection does not extend to a deputy sheriff.[54]

ute, a threat to make an unlawful arrest. "A seaman who has shipped or entered into a contract for a voyage from a port in this Commonwealth shall not be liable to arrest on mesne process on account of a debt to a landlord or boarding house keeper." Rev. Laws of Mass. c. 66, § 4. A sheriff is exempt, by Rev. Laws of Mass. c. 23, § 10, from arrest at any time on mesne process or execution in a civil action.

[54] George v. Fellows, 58 N. H. 494.

CHAPTER XIII

FALSE IMPRISONMENT

§ 271. Definition. — Any unlawful restraint of a person contrary to his will,[1] either with or without process of law, is a false imprisonment,[2] and makes the restraining offender liable to the State in a criminal action, and to the imprisoned one in a civil action.

§ 272. Restraint must be against the Will. — The restraint must be without the consent of the imprisoned party, and a child of tender years may not be able to give such consent as will make the imprisonment lawful.[3]

§ 273. Restraint must be Total. — The restraint must be a total one. Compelling a man to go in a given direction against his will may amount to an imprisonment, and if it is an *entire* restraint, there certainly is an imprisonment. So if an officer commands a person to go with him, and the orders are

---

[1] Com. v. Nickerson, 5 Allen (Mass.), 518.

[2] Comer v. Knowles, 17 Kan. 436; Brewster v. People, 183 Ill. 146.

[3] Com. v. Nickerson, supra cit.

obeyed, and they go in the direction pointed out by the officer, that is an imprisonment, though no actual violence be used, and though there is not even a touching of the person; it is enough that there is a complete control of the person's liberty, and a submission by him.

But restraining a man from going in a particular direction, at the same time leaving one direction open and free for him to go if he choose, does not constitute an imprisonment, because there is no *total* restraint of his freedom.[4]

§ 274. **Restraint may be by Words.** — In ordinary practice, words are sufficient to constitute an imprisonment, if they impose a restraint upon the person, and the party is accordingly restrained; for he is not obliged to incur the risk of personal violence and insult by resisting until actual violence be used. This principle is reasonable in itself, and is fully sustained by the authorities.

§ 275. **Having in Power is sufficient.** — Nor does there seem that there should be any very formal declaration of arrest. If the officer goes for the purpose of executing his warrant, has the party in his presence and power, if the party so understands it, and in consequence thereof submits, and the officer, in the execution of the warrant, takes the party before a magistrate, or receives money or property in

---

[4] Bird *v.* Jones, 7 Q. B. (Eng.) 742.

discharge of his person, it is in law an arrest, although he did not touch any part of the body.[5]

§ 276. **Touching not Necessary to complete Offence.** — It is not necessary to constitute false imprisonment that the person restrained of his liberty should be touched or actually arrested. If he is ordered to do or not to do the thing, to move or not to move against his own free will, — if it is not left to his option to go or stay where he pleases, and force is offered, or there is reasonable ground to apprehend that coercive measures will be used if he does not yield,[6] the offence is complete upon his submission.

A false imprisonment may be committed by words alone, or by acts alone, or by both, and by merely operating on the will of the individual, or by personal violence, or both. It is not necessary that the individual be confined within a prison or within walls, or that he be assaulted or even touched.[7]

It may be committed by threats,[8] but it is not necessary that it be a malicious act, or that the slightest wrongful intention exist.[9]

§ 277. **Must be a Threat or Show of Force.** — Proof that the defendant induced the plaintiff to go

---

[5] Pike v. Hanson, 9 N. H. 491.

[6] Johnson v. Tompkins, 1 Baldwin (U. S. C. C.), 571.

[7] Comer v. Knowles, 17 Kan. 435.

[8] Herring v. State, 3 Tex. App. 108; Meyer v. State, 49 S. W. (Tex.) 600.

[9] Comer v. Knowles, supra cit.

to another place, and there remain in concealment for a time, by threats of a criminal prosecution and misrepresentations, but without using or threatening to use force, is not sufficient to maintain the action.[10]

§ 278. **Warrant valid in Form, from Court of General Jurisdiction, protects Officer.** — As a general rule, to secure immunity from liability, the officer is bound only to see that the process which he is called upon to execute is in due and regular form, and issues from a court having general jurisdiction of the subject. In such case he is justified in obeying his precept. And it is highly necessary to the due, prompt, and energetic execution of the commands of the law that he should be so.[11]

Therefore an officer who has an execution from a court of competent jurisdiction is not liable for arresting a defendant who shows his discharge in insolvency to the officer before he is arrested.[12]

An officer cannot stop to try the validity of such a certificate of discharge when he is about to serve a legal process, and to so hold would defeat the service.

§ 279. **Serving Lawful Process Improperly.** — Serving lawful process in an unauthorized manner constitutes false imprisonment.[13]

[10] Payson v. Macomber, 3 Allen (Mass.), 69.
[11] McMahan v. Green, 34 Vt. 69.
[12] Wilmarth v. Burt, 7 Metc. (Mass.) 257.
[13] Wood v. Graves, 144 Mass. 365.

A person who causes another to be arrested on mesne process in a civil action is liable to an action of false imprisonment, if he fails to first make an affidavit that is required by statute.[14]

If an arrest under a lawful warrant be made for the purpose of extorting money, or to unlawfully enforce the payment of a civil claim, an action of false imprisonment will lie against all who have, either directly or indirectly, participated therein.[15] But procuring a warrant by misrepresentations does not make the party so procuring the warrant liable to an action for false imprisonment.[16] Nor does legally enforcing the payment of a debt by means of an arrest, constitute the offence.[17]

On an execution against a corporation, styled the president, directors, and company of a turnpike, the officer was held liable for the arrest and detention of one of the proprietors; because the party arrested was neither named nor described in the writ, the corporate name not being the name or description of any natural person whomsoever, therefore he did that which his precept did not authorize him to do, when he made the arrest.[18]

---

[14] Cody v. Adams, 7 Gray (Mass.), 59.

[15] Hackett v. King, 6 Allen (Mass.), 58; Vanderpool v. State, 34 Ark. 174; Slomer v. People, 25 Ill. 61; Neufeld v. Rodeminski, 144 Ill. 88.

[16] Coupal v. Ward, 106 Mass. 289.

[17] Mullen v. Brown, 138 Mass. 114.

[18] Nichols v. Thomas, 4 Mass. 232.

§ 280. **Discharging Prisoner without taking before Magistrate.** — To arrest a man for being drunk and disorderly, and then discharge him without taking him before a magistrate, constitutes the offence, unless the prisoner waived his right to be so taken, by consenting to the discharge.[19]

§ 281. **Subsequent Arrest for Offence committed in Presence of Officer.** — Where an officer arrests an intoxicated person, while guilty of disorderly conduct, and releases him on his promise to go directly home, he may lawfully retake him, on his going into a barroom before he is out of the officer's sight, and is not guilty of false imprisonment in so doing; and it makes no difference whether the final restraint be considered a recaption, or a new arrest for disorderly conduct still continuing.[20]

§ 282. **Imprisoned Party must be Conscious of Restraint.** — To constitute an imprisonment, the party imprisoned must be conscious of the restraint.[21] So where a schoolmaster, improperly, and under a claim for money due for schooling, refused to allow the mother of an infant scholar to take her son home with her, and the son, though frequently demanded by the mother, was kept at the school,

---

[19] Brock v. Stimson, 108 Mass. 520.
[20] Com. v. Hastings, 9 Metc. (Mass.) 262.
[21] Herring v. Boyle, 1 Cromp. M. & R. (Eng. Exch.) 377.

there being no proof that the boy knew of the demand and denial, or that any restraint had been imposed upon him, it was held, when he brought an action for false imprisonment, that it was not maintainable.[22]

[22] Herring *v.* Boyle, 1 Cromp. M. & R. (Eng. Exch.) 377.

CHAPTER XIV

TRESPASS

§ 283. **Definition.** — A trespass is any misfeasance, — that is, the doing of a lawful act in an unlawful manner, — or act of one man whereby another is injuriously treated or damaged,[1] either in his person, his property, or his rights. And a trespasser has been defined to be one who does an unlawful act, or a lawful act in an unlawful manner, to the injury of the person or property of another.[2]

§ 284. **Trespass Vi et Armis.** — A trespass committed with force, as, for example, striking another unlawfully, is said to be done *vi et armis* (with force and arms).

§ 285. **Accidental Acts.** — As the ground of compensation is the injury done, a civil action lies for an unintentional act of trespass, even if there is no malice;[3] but not always for an accidental act.[4]

---

[1] 3 Bl. Com. 208.
[2] Bouvier's Law Dict. (Trespasser).
[3] Bigelow *v.* Stearns, 19 Johns. (N. Y.) 38.
[4] Brown *v.* Kendall, 6 Cush. (Mass.) 292; Vincent *v.* Stinehour, 7 Vt. 62; Hobart *v.* Hagget, 12 Me. 67; Blewitt *v.* Phillips, 1 Q. B. (Eng.) 86.

Such accidental act, however, will not excuse a trespass, unless the act be unintentional, unavoidable, and without the least fault on the part of the trespasser.[5]

§ 286. **Criminal Intent Necessary to Criminal Action.** — But a *criminal* action for trespass does not lie unless the trespass be done with a criminal intent,[6] — that is, an intent to commit a crime. A criminal intent does not necessarily mean that a knowledge of wrong doing must exist, for it has been held that a mere knowledge of the facts of the case will supply this intent;[7] and it is immaterial whether the person who committed the offence knew that it was in violation of the law.

§ 287. **Officer not Chargeable with Errors of Magistrate.** — An officer is never liable for the regular enforcement of legal process which contains errors made by the issuing magistrate, provided the process is regular on its face.[8]

§ 288. **Unauthorized Entrance of Officer is at his Peril.** — An officer armed with civil process, who enters upon premises without invitation of the occupant thereof, who has done no act to induce the officer to reasonably believe that the party whom he

---

[5] Jennings v. Fundeburg, 4 McCord (S. C.), 161.
[6] Bessey v. Olliott, T. Raym. (Eng. K. B.) 467.
[7] U. S. v. Anthony, 11 Blatchf. (U. S. C. C.) 200.
[8] Stutsman County v. Wallace, 142 U. S. 293.

seeks to serve is there, is a trespasser, if the person whom he seeks is not a resident there, or there in fact.[9]

§ 289. **Statutory Authority must be followed Strictly.** — An officer who makes an arrest by authority of a statute, must follow the statute strictly, or he becomes a trespasser. As where an officer arrests an intoxicated person under authority of a statute which provides that the officer shall take the arrested person " before some justice of the peace, or police court in the city or town wherein he has been found, and shall make complaint against him for the crime of drunkenness," is guilty of trespass if he takes him before a justice in another town,[10] if there is a justice in the town where he is found, or if he releases him without taking him before a justice at all.[11] And an officer is never liable for an act done under the authority of a constitutional statute;[12] otherwise if the statute is unconstitutional.

§ 290. **Arrest for Intoxication.** — If an officer, without a warrant, arrests a person for being intoxicated, he does so at his peril; that is, if the person so arrested is not in fact intoxicated, the

[9] Blatt v. McBarron, 161 Mass. 21.
[10] Papineau v. Bacon, 110 Mass. 319.
[11] Brock v. Stimson, 108 Mass. 520; State v. Parker, 75 N. C. 249.
[12] Brown v. Beatty, 34 Miss. 227.

officer is guilty of trespass, for nothing but clear proof of the intoxication will justify the arrest. The fact that the arrest was made in good faith, and under a reasonable belief of the intoxication, will not excuse the trespass.[13] And it is immaterial how the intoxication was produced.[14] But an officer is not liable *criminally* for arresting a person who is subsequently shown not to have been intoxicated at the time of the arrest.[15]

§ 291. **Liability of Party assisting an Officer.** — There seems to be some doubt whether a private person who, at the command of an officer, assists him in making an arrest, is guilty of trespass, if the process in the hands of the officer is not regular and valid. The cases which hold that the private person called upon under such circumstances is not liable, seem to be founded upon the better reasoning. It is certainly neither law nor accurate reasoning to assume that a person upon whom the performance of a duty is thrown by law, as it is when a known officer commands assistance in making an arrest, and who is subject to a criminal prosecution if he does not obey the command of the law,[16] is

[13] Phillips *v.* Fadden, 125 Mass. 198.
[14] Com. *v.* Coughlin, 123 Mass. 436.
[15] Com. *v.* Cheney, 141 Mass. 102. But see State *v.* Hunter, 106 N. C. 796.
[16] Coyles *v.* Hurtin, 10 Johns. (N. Y.) 84; Watson *v.* State, 83 Ala. 60; Dougherty *v.* State, 106 Ala. 63; McMahan *v.* Green, 34 Vt. 69; Pruitt *v.* Miller, 3 Ind. 16; Firestone *v.* Rice, 71 Mich. 377.

not fully protected by the law in the performance of that duty.

A fair statement of the law applicable in such cases would seem to be, that one who, at the *command* of an officer, assists him in the execution of legal process, is fully protected, although the process is not regular and valid; but if he acts of his own volition, he must show that the process is valid, in order to justify his act.[17]

But where the original act of the officer is wrongful in itself, as it would be if the officer, without a warrant, were to arrest one for a past misdemeanor, any stranger who aids him in it will be liable to the party injured, although he acts by the officer's command.

§ 292. **Bystander may be justified in not Responding.** — A bystander is not obliged to respond to an officer's command of assistance unless there is a reasonable necessity. He may also set up physical impossibility or other lawful excuse in defence.[18]

---

[17] Reed *v.* Rice, 2 J. J. Marshall (Ky.), 44; State *v.* Stalcup, 1 Ired. (N. C.) 30; McMahan *v.* Green, 34 Vt. 69; Firestone *v.* Rice, 71 Mich. 377; Watson *v.* State, 83 Ala. 60. *Contra:* Elder *v.* Morrison, 10 Wend. (N. Y.) 128; Hooker *v.* Smith, 19 Vt. 151; Mitchell *v.* State, 12 Ark. 50; Dietrichs *v.* Schaw, 43 Ind. 175. See also Dehm *v.* Hinman, 56 Conn. 320.

[18] Reg. *v.* Brown, Car. & M. 314; State *v.* Deniston, 6 Blackf. (Ind.) 277.

§ 293. **Unlawful Arrest ordered by Third Party.** — An unlawful arrest ordered by a third person makes such person liable in damages.[19]

Trespass ab Initio.

§ 294. **Arises from Abuse of Legal Authority.** — An officer who in serving civil process, or making a civil arrest, does any act which he has no right to do, or does an act in an unlawful manner which he might be justified in doing if he did it in a lawful manner, becomes thereby a trespasser *ab initio* (from the beginning); that is, every act in connection with the service of the process which was lawful when done, by doing that single unlawful act, becomes thereby unlawful.[20] But the officer's assistant is not affected by a subsequent abuse of process.[21]

The entry must be by authority of law, or the officer cannot become a trespasser *ab initio*. The subsequent act, however, will not make the officer a trespasser *ab initio*, unless it shows a purpose to use his legal entry as the cover for the wrongful act, or unless the subsequent wrongful act is in itself a trespass.[22]

---

[19] King *v.* Ward, 77 Ill. 603; Taafe *v.* Slevin, 11 Mo. App. 507.

[20] Com. *v.* Tobin, 108 Mass. 426.

[21] Oystead *v.* Shed, 12 Mass. 505; Wheelock *v.* Archer, 26 Vt. 380.

[22] Shorland *v.* Govett, 5 B. & C. (Eng. K. B.) 485.

§ 295. **Application of the Doctrine.** — The doctrine of trespass *ab initio* does not apply to criminal cases.[23] Nor does it apply when the entry is by permission of the party, as where an officer enters, not by authority of law, but by permission of the party, and then wrongfully takes possession of certain papers; there the original entry was not a trespass.[24]

[23] Com. v. Tobin, 108 Mass. 426.
[24] Allen v. Crofutt, 5 Wend. (N. Y.) 506.

INDEX

[References are to sections.]

A.

AFFIDAVIT,
    is necessary to civil arrest, 107.
    what must be stated in the, 107
    new, is necessary if writ is altered, 108.
    failure to make may be cause of action, 279.

ALTERING WARRANT,
    effect of, 108.
    may be done only by issuing magistrate, 48.

AMBASSADORS (*See* MINISTER, CONSULS),
    or attendants cannot be arrested, 256.

ARREST (*See* OFFICER, PRISONER, WARRANT, PROCESS, RESTRAINT, SUNDAY, FALSE IMPRISONMENT, TRESPASS),
    what constitutes, 65.
    requisites of legal, 66.
    made in four ways, 20.
    officer must make known his authority to, 78.
    authority to, may be known by circumstances, 85.
    by known officer is notice of authority, 81.
    authority and duty to, are coincident, 183.
    constructive notice of authority to, 85.
    under general authority, 146.
    want of authority to, will not protect prisoner from prosecution, 14, 15.
    may not be made on Sunday in civil case, 47, 76.
    for vagrancy, 142.
    for conspiracy may be on Sunday, 261.
    on criminal charge may be at any time, 76.

[References are to sections.]

ARREST — *Continued.*
    in criminal case may be made anywhere, 77.
    importance of consummation of the arrest, 68.
    may be by words alone, 66, 73.
    touching may be necessary to, 69, 73.
    consummated by touching, though accused flee, 74.
    restraint always necessary to, 73.
    taking into custody necessary to, 71, 73.
    force in making, 183, 185–188.
    killing in making, 86, 92, 144, 145, 183, 184, 187–189.
    in wanton and menacing manner, 86.
    right to kill when fleeing from, 144, 145, 189.
    without warrant, 112 *et seq.*
    without warrant when one is required, 6.
    for violation of city ordinances, 131.
    without warrant for breach of peace must be immediate, 141, 142.
    for breach of peace, 76, 116.
    by private person for breach of peace, 116.
    by officer for breach of peace, 129.
    while committing breach of the peace, 116, 141, 142.
    in case of misdemeanor, by private person, 116.
    in case of felony, by private person, 112, 155.
    bail may arrest principal without warrant anywhere, 148.
    with warrant is preferable, 20.
    with warrant, 90 *et seq.*
    cannot be of party not named or described in warrant, 90, 279.
    may be an old warrant not returned, 35.
    under lawful warrant for improper purpose, 279.
    mere reading warrant is not sufficient to constitute, 67.
    officer may be acting in, though at distance, 75.
    by officer outside of jurisdiction, 135.
    within house by officer outside, 158.
    may be by officer's assistant, 75.
    duty to submit to illegal, by known officer, 92.
    may be by excepting alternative, 72.

INDEX

[References are to sections.]

ARREST — *Continued.*
    in night, 76.
    in different county, 49.
    on reasonable suspicion, 129.
    for contempt of court, 64.
    for contempt of legislative body, 63.
    to prevent crime, 149.
    for fraud, 137.
    in civil cases, 103–111.
    statute authorizing civil, 104.
    officer's duty after making, 87.
    exemption from, 256 *et seq.*

ASSISTANCE,
    private person may be entitled to, 113.
    criminal offence to refuse officer, 291.
    defences to charge of refusing officer, 292.

ASSISTANT,
    arrest may be by, 75.
    of officer may be liable, 95.

AUTHORITY (*See* NOTICE),
    notice of, to arrest, 78, 81.
    to arrest may be known by circumstances, 85.
    officer must make known, to arrest, 78.
    constructive notice of, to arrest, 85.
    arrest under general, 146.
    and duty to arrest are coincident, 183.
    in writing bail may delegate, to arrest, 148.
    burden of proof to show, to arrest, 235.

B.

BAIL,
    excessive, shall not be required, 5.
    one under, in extradition has no opportunity to leave State, 220.
    in writing may delegate authority to arrest principal, 148.
    may arrest principal without warrant anywhere, 148.
    may break doors to arrest principal, 148.

[References are to sections.]

BENCH WARRANT,
    what is a, 26.
    purpose of the term, 26.

BILL OF RIGHTS,
    American, 6.
    English, 5.

BREACH OF THE PEACE,
    what is, 117.
    essence of the offence, 119.
    includes all indictable offences, 261.
    arrest for, 76. 116.
    arrest while committing, 116, 141, 142.
    arrest for, without warrant, must be immediate, 141, 142.
    arrest by private person for, 116.
    arrest by officer for, 129.
    entering unfastened door to arrest for, 138.
    entering fastened door to arrest for, 139.
    inciting others to break the peace is a, 118.
    calling names opprobriously may be, 118, 125.
    no defence to charge of, that opprobrious words are true, 119.
    abating nuisance in unlawful manner is, 120.
    loud and violent abusive language is a, 121.
    wanton discharge of a firearm may be, 122.
    doing lawful act in a turbulent manner is a, 120.
    threatening officer may be a, 121.
    disturbance of public worship is a, 123.
    soliciting by a prostitute is a, 124.
    reckless driving is a, 126.
    profane swearing may be a, 127.
    shouting in streets at night may be a, 126.
    public and disorderly drunkenness may be a, 127.
    to constitute, must disturb an indefinite number of persons, 125.

BREAKING (*See* DOOR, HOUSE),
    what is a, 172.
    injury of material not necessary to a, 173.

INDEX

[References are to sections.]

BREAKING — *Continued.*
    removing anything relied on as security, is a, 173, 180.
    when justifiable, 144, 145, 147, 152 *et seq.*
    breaking doors, 175.
    breaking windows, 176.
    by making or entering other openings, 177.
    enlarging opening by actual, 178.
    by removing iron grating over sidewalk, 180.
    entrance under deception may be, 181.
    taking advantage of negligence of occupant is not, 174, 177.
    right of private person to break, 155.
    bail may break to arrest principal, 148.
    not, to open inner doors, 162.
    unannounced entrance to make original arrest is an unjustifiable, 159.
    notification, demand, and refusal necessary before, 153, 159.
    need not always give name of party sought before, 154.
    to prevent escape, 157.
    effect of arrest by unlawful, 182.

BURDEN OF PROOF (*See* EVIDENCE),
    is with the prosecution, 229.
    never shifts from the prosecution, 229–231.
    as to new and distinct proposition, 130, 131.
    in showing license to sell, 236.
    respecting criminal capacity of children, 249.
    in insanity, 237.
    as to voluntary character of confession, 245.
    when charge is use of excessive force, 233.
    on officer to show offence committed in presence, 234.
    to show authority to arrest, 235.

C.

CHARACTER,
    good, always admissible, 240.
    bad, may be admissible, 238.

[References are to sections.]

CHARACTER — *Continued.*
    evidence must be of general repute, 239.
    how proven, 241.
    at present time is of most importance, 241.
    evidence must be of particular trait in question, 239.

CHILDREN,
    under seven years cannot commit crime, 249.
    between seven and fourteen years may be unable to commit crime, 249.

CLUB,
    officer's right to use, 191, 192.
    may use, if necessary to stop fight, 191.
    may not use, if prisoner merely holds back, 191.
    unjustified assault with, 193.

COMPLAINT (*See* OATH, AFFIDAVIT),
    required by constitution, 23.
    who may make, 53.
    need not be in writing except by statute, 54.
    if insufficient may render officer liable, 33.

COMPLAINING PARTY,
    may be a trespasser if magistrate has no jurisdiction, 16.

CONFESSION,
    is admissible if voluntary, 245.
    must be made to whom, 244, 245.
    must go in entire, 246.
    by intoxicated person, 244.
    is open to explanation, 246.
    although not admissible, collateral information may be, 247.

CONFINING PRISONER,
    in State penitentiary, 100.
    in unhealthful place, 100.
    freight car may be used for, 100.
    length of time in, 195.
    force may be used in, 198.

CONSTITUTIONAL PROVISIONS,
    respecting search warrants, 23.

[References are to sections.]

CONSTITUTIONAL PROVISIONS — *Continued*.
    do not apply to searches by State authorities, 23.
    respecting description of arrested party, 41.
    prohibit physical examination by compulsion, 203.
    respecting rendition, 222.
    respecting "due process of law," 6.
    respecting jury trials, 6, 7.
    respecting arrest for debt, 103.
    respecting probable cause and oath, 52, 57.

CONSTITUTIONAL RIGHT,
    to jury trial cannot be waived, 7.

CONSUL GENERALS,
    are exempt from arrest, 257.

CONSULS,
    are not exempt from arrest, 257.

CONTEMPT,
    arrest for contempt of court, 64.
    arrest of party or witness at court is a contempt, 264.
    arrest for contempt of legislative body, 63.

COURT,
    arrest in, 77, 264.

CRIMINAL INTENT,
    what is a, 286.
    is necessary to a crime, 248.
    and criminal act must concur, 248.

CUSTODY,
    taking into, necessary to arrest, 71, 73.

D.

DEBTOR
    arrest of, about to leave State, 105.
    affidavit necessary to arrest of, 107, 279.
    intent to defraud necessary to arrest of, 106.
    may be exempt from arrest, 269.
    effect of altering writ for arrest of, 108.
    no arrest of, after attachment of property, 109.
    filing petition in insolvency after arrest, 111.

[References are to sections.]

DELAY,
    in making an arrest for a breach of the peace, 141, 142.
    in taking prisoner before a magistrate, 96, 195.

DESERTERS (*See* MILITARY LAW).

DOOR (*See* BREAKING, HOUSE),
    breaking, 175.
    breaking in pursuit of felon, 144.
    right of private person to break, 155.
    bail may break to arrest principal, 148.
    military officer may not break to arrest deserter, 147.
    entering unfastened, to arrest for breach of peace, 138.
    entering fastened to arrest for breach of the peace, 139.
    mere protective, is not legal outer door, 179.
    inner, may be legal outer door, 162, 163.
    inner, may be broken on any process, 162.

DOUBT,
    always goes to benefit of the accused, 231, 254.

DRUNKENNESS (*See* INTOXICATION),
    may be a breach of the peace, 127.
    will excuse delay in taking before a magistrate, 96.
    may be a defence to a criminal charge, 243.

DUE PROCESS OF LAW,
    what is, 6.
    constitutional provisions respecting, 6.

DWELLING HOUSE (*See* HOUSE),
    what is a, 164.
    to constitute, must be used for sleeping purposes, 170.
    use of, determines character, 165.
    use of portion as, 166.
    combined place of business and, 169.
    may be several, in same building, 167.
    public building may be a, 168.
    must be occupied for purpose of, 165.
    effect of absence on character of, 171.

DYING DECLARATIONS,
    why admissible, 250.
    may be oral, written, or by signs, 250.

[References are to sections.]

DYING DECLARATIONS — *Continued.*
    party making, must expect immediate death, 251.
    must be made by one who, if living, would be competent, 252.
    young child cannot make, 252.

E.

ELECTION,
    one going to or returning from, is exempt from civil arrest, 268.
    one merely preparing to go to, is not exempt, 268.

ENDORSING WARRANT,
    to arrest in another county, 49.

ESCAPE,
    what is, 88.
    may be a felony or misdemeanor, 89.
    accused may be re-taken on same warrant, or without warrant, 89.
    officer is responsible for, 89, 194.
    on void warrant there cannot be, 89.
    cannot be unless arrest is consummated, 68.
    innocence or guilt of party escaping is not material, 89.
    use of force in preventing, 187, 188, 194.
    in pursuit for, unannounced entrance into house is justifiable, 160.
    breaking into house to prevent, 157.
    anything may be taken from prisoner that may be used in, 200.

ESTOPPEL,
    doctrine of, does not apply to criminal cases, 246.

EVIDENCE (*See* BURDEN OF PROOF, CONFESSIONS, CHARACTER, DYING DECLARATIONS),
    conduct as, of guilt, 242.
    of character, 238–241.
    preponderance is not sufficient, 228.
    must not be obtained by compulsory physical examination, 203.

INDEX

[References are to sections.]

EVIDENCE — *Continued.*
    prisoner's silence weighed against him, 242.
    destroying evidence, 242.
    destroying marks of ownership, 242.
    of use of threats, 242.
    of taking to flight, 242.
    disguise, 242.
    concealment, 242.
    possession of stolen goods as, 242a.
    presumption of innocence is not, 232, 236.
    degree of, to warrant holding in extradition, 211.
    collateral, obtained by confession is admissible, 247
    obtained by illegal seizure is competent, 24a.
    best, only is competent, 253.
    hearsay evidence not admissible, 253.

EXEMPTION FROM ARREST,
    in general, 256 *et seq.*
    ambassadors are, 256.
    sovereign of friendly foreign nation is, 256.
    any diplomatic agent of friendly foreign nation is, 256.
    Consul Generals are, 257.
    consuls are not, 257.
    attorneys at law are, 258.
    persons under guardianship, 266.
    bail are, 259.
    bankrupts are, and insolvents may be, 259.
    clergymen, 259.
    militia men, 259.
    electors, 259.
    jurors, 259.
    sheriffs and other peace officers, 259, 270.
    employee of the United States may not be, 260.
    driver of mail wagon may not be, 260.
    members of Congress, 261.
    extends to one denied seat, 268.
    State legislators, 261.
    does not extend to expelled or merely elected member, 261.

INDEX 185

[References are to sections.]

EXEMPTION FROM ARREST— *Continued.*
    witnesses and parties to suits, 264.
    may usually be waived, 262.
    may not be waived by attorney or legislator, 262.
    may be waived by a party to a court proceeding, 265.
    voluntary witness is not exempt, 264.
    officer is not liable for arresting exempt party, 267.
    includes going to and returning from certain places, 268.
    by statute, 269, 270.

EXTRADITION (*See* RENDITION),
    and rendition distinguished, 204.
    definition of, 205.
    who may issue warrant in, 207, 208.
    usual method of procedure in, 215.
    sanction of demand necessary to give jurisdiction, 214.
    is matter of treaty or comity, 206, 216, 226.
    no comity on part of United States, 217.
    is obligatory between States of the United States, 226.
    requisites of warrant in, 209.
    degree of evidence to warrant holding in, 211.
    negotiations in, must be by highest executive officers, 214.
    guilt or innocence not inquired into on habeas corpus in, 213.
    re-arrest after discharge on habeas corpus in, 210.
    re-arrest after discharge on merits, 218.
    taking before a magistrate in, 211.
    for what crimes a fugitive may be tried in, 218, 219.
    kidnapped fugitive may be tried for any offence, 219.

F.

FACT,
    ignorance of, may excuse, 32.

FALSE IMPRISONMENT (*See* ARREST, TRESPASS),
    definition of, 271.
    may be by mere words, 273, 274, 276.

[References are to sections.]

FALSE IMPRISONMENT—*Continued.*
    must be against will, 272.
    to constitute, there must be a total restraint, 273.
    none unless party is conscious of restraint, 275, 282.
    touching of person not necessary to, 273-276.
    there must be at least a threat or show of force, 277.
    may be by serving process improperly, 279.

FELONY (*See* ARREST, OFFICER, PRIVATE PERSON),
    what is a, 115.
    escape may be a, 89.
    arrest for, may be made on Sunday, 47, 76.
    killing to prevent, 128, 144.
    right of private person to arrest for, 112, 155.
    right of officer to arrest for, 129.
    may kill if necessary in arresting for, 144, 145.

FORCE (*See* KILLING, CLUB),
    use of, in making an arrest, 183, 185-188.
    officer is liable for excessive, 190.
    may be used in confining prisoner, 198.
    may be used in searching prisoner, 201.
    use of, to prevent escape, 187, 188, 194.
    burden of proof in charge of use of excessive, 233.

FRESH PURSUIT (*See* KILLING, BREAKING, DOOR),
    may justify private person in breaking doors, 145, 155.
    on, pursuer may kill if necessary to prevent escape, 145.

FUGITIVE FROM JUSTICE,
    who is a, 227.

G.

GOVERNMENT,
    limit of right to control, 9.

H.

HABEAS CORPUS,
    history of, 4.
    guilt or innocence not inquired into on, 213.
    re-arrest after discharge under writ of, 210.

INDEX 187

[References are to sections.]

HANDCUFFS,
 when use of, is justifiable, 194, 198.
 right to use, depends on circumstances, 194, 198.
 right to use, on party arrested in a civil suit, 198.
 must not be used to join convicted to unconvicted person, 194.
 use of, rests with discretion of officer, 194, 198.
 may be used when a rescue is expected, 194.

HOUSE (*See* BREAKING, DOOR, DWELLING HOUSE),
 is castle, 151.
 cannot usually be broken to serve civil process, 152.
 may be broken to serve criminal process, 152.
 to whom the protection of, is extended, 156.

HUE AND CRY,
 what is, 150.
 arrest under, is justifiable though no felony committed, 114.

I.

IGNORANCE OF THE LAW,
 is usually no excuse, 31, 255.
 if regarding ownership, may excuse larceny, 255.

IMPOSSIBILITY,
 may excuse officer from obeying command of law, 99.

INFANT,
 under seven cannot commit crime, 249.
 between seven and fourteen prima facie incapable of crime, 249.

INNOCENCE,
 presumption of, 232, 236.
 presumption has no weight as evidence, 232.
 effect of presumption, 232.
 when presumption disappears from case, 232.

INTERFERENCE (*See* RESISTING),
 by third persons may be lawful, 94.
 officer may not club one who merely interferes, 192.

188 INDEX

[References are to sections.]

INTOXICATION (*See* DRUNKENNESS),
    may be a defence, 243.
    immaterial how produced, 290.
    officer arrests for, at his peril, 290.
    destroys admissibility of confession, 244.
    will not justify searching the prisoner, 202.
    will excuse delay in taking prisoner before magistrate, 96.

J.

JURISDICTION (*See* MAGISTRATE, PROCESS, WARRANT),
    lack of, if of person, may not invalidate process, 16.
    no immunity because of enticing into, 14.
    obtained by illegal arrest, or kidnapping, 14, 15.
    over foreign vessels, 18.
    over ceded territory, 19.
    statute giving, implies power to apprehend, 59.
    officer must know that magistrate has general, 29.
    if magistrate has none, process is wholly void, 16.
    in absence of, all parties are trespassers, 16.

JURY,
    public trial by, is necessary in certain cases, 6.
    trial by, cannot be waived, 7.

K.

KILLING (*See* FORCE, FELONY),
    when justifiable in making arrest, 144, 145, 183.
    Blackstone's rule regarding, in making arrest, 184.
    if necessary to arrest in felony, 144, 145.
    to prevent escape in felony, 187.
    to prevent escape in misdemeanor, 188.
    to prevent felony, 128, 144.
    in resisting arrest, 86, 92.
    when fleeing from arrest, 144, 145, 189.

INDEX 189

[References are to sections.]

L.

LIFE (*See* KILLING, FORCE),
    taking of, in arresting, 86, 92, 128, 144, 145, 183, 187–189.

M.

MAGISTRATE (*See* PROCESS, WARRANT),
    must follow law in issuing process, 11.
    cannot justify under authority of an unconstitutional statute, 16.
    must have general jurisdiction of subject matter, 16, 29.
    effect of lack of jurisdiction in, 16.
    issuing, need not have trial jurisdiction, 28.
    may be trespasser for acting without authority, 16.
    officer is not chargeable with errors of, 287.
    officer should take prisoner before, 96, 102.
    may delay in taking prisoner before, for cause, 96.
    drunkenness will excuse delay in taking before, 96.
    prisoner may waive his right to be taken before, 102, 280.
    issuing warrant only may alter it, 48.

MAGNA CHARTA,
    secured right of personal liberty, 3.
    is written evidence of right of personal liberty, 3.

MANDAMUS,
    may lie to compel justice to take action, 51.

MILITARY LAW,
    offender against, must not be arrested without warrant, 147.
    military officer may not break outer door to arrest deserter, 147.

MINISTER (*See* AMBASSADOR),
    foreign, cannot be arrested, 256.
    legation attaché is a, 256.
    foreign, cannot waive privilege of exemption, 256.
    citizen may exercise right of self-defence against foreign, 256.

190 INDEX

[References are to sections.]

MISDEMEANOR,
arrest for, by private person, 116.
escape may be, 89.

MISTAKE,
if clerical, may not render officer liable, 33.

N.

NAME,
of party or description is necessary in warrant, 39, 45, 279.
use of fictitious, in warrant, 40.
party known by several names, 43.

NECESSITY,
as excuse for acting or not acting, 101.
what is "reasonable necessity," 101.

NIGHT,
arrest may be in, 76.

NOTICE (*See* AUTHORITY),
of authority to arrest, 78, 81-85.
need not be given to outsiders, 84.

O.

OATH (*See* COMPLAINT, AFFIDAVIT),
is necessary to issue of a warrant, 56, 57, 107, 279.
that oath was made must appear on face of warrant, 93.

OFFICER (*See* ARREST, PROCESS, WARRANT, CLUB),
may be trespasser for lack of jurisdiction in issuing magistrate, 16.
cannot justify act under unconstitutional statute, 16.
how far protected by warrant valid upon its face, 30.
is protected by valid warrant, 91, 278.
must serve void warrant, if valid on its face, 33.
warrant no protection to, if invalid on its face, 92.
is protected in serving void warrant, if defect is not on face, 33.
is charged with two duties to secure immunity, 29.

INDEX

[References are to sections.]

OFFICER — *Continued.*
    may be liable if complaint is not sufficient, 33.
    not liable for arresting exempted person, 267.
    not chargeable with errors of issuing magistrate, 287.
    may deputize another to serve as assistant, 62.
    may be considered as acting in arrest though at distance, 75.
    assistant of, may be liable if officer is, 95.
    may command assistance, 110.
    must have warrant with him when arresting, 46.
    assistant of, may make arrest, 75.
    liability of party assisting, 291.
    bystander may refuse assistance to, 292.
    may sometimes arrest outside of jurisdiction, 135.
    finding impossible to perform is excused, 99.
    when justified in using own judgment, 101.
    must exhibit authority, if demanded, 82.
    need not imperil warrant, 79.
    duty of, after making arrest, 87, 195.
    must rely on name alone in warrant, 40.
    one not a known, must show his warrant, 82.
    effect of failure to exhibit authority, 80.
    duty to submit to illegal arrest by known, 92.
    right of, to arrest for felony, 129.
    may arrest on reasonable suspicion of felony, 129.
    once lawfully in house may re-enter forcibly, 161.
    may arrest without warrant, 129.
    unauthorized entrance of, at his peril, 288.
    arrest within house by, outside, 158.
    is liable for use of excessive force, 190.
    right of, to use club, 191.
    may not use club on one who merely interferes, 192.
    unlawful act of, deprives him of protection of law, 193.
    demanding number of, 192.
    responsibility for escape, 89, 194.
    arrests for intoxication at his peril, 290.
    not liable for clerical mistake, 33.
    may be exempt from arrest, 259, 270.

INDEX

[References are to sections.]

OFFICER — *Continued.*
    threatening, may be a breach of the peace, 121.
    right of, to detain prisoner, 98.
    right of, to release prisoner, 97, 197, 280, 281.
    when custody of prisoner ceases, 197.

P.

PERSONAL LIBERTY,
    right of, 1.
    demands restraint, 8.
    was secured by Magna Charta, 3.
    was strengthened by subsequent acts, 4.
    is a natural right, 2.
    no one to be deprived of, without due process of law, 6.

PETITION OF RIGHT,
    provision of, 4.

PLACE OF ARREST,
    may be anywhere on a criminal charge, 77.

POSSESSION,
    of stolen goods as evidence, 242a.

PRESENCE,
    what is, 134.
    burden is on officer to show, 234.
    by special authority may arrest for offence not committed in, 132.

PRISONER,
    is not entitled to immunity because enticed into jurisdiction, 14.
    officer has no right to roughly use the, 186.
    must not be forced to a physical examination, 203.
    right to search, 200.
    mere intoxication will not justify searching, 202.
    force may be used in confining, 198.
    must be confined in a suitable place, 100.
    disposing of, 96.
    may be searched at time of arrest, 202.

[References are to sections.]

PRISONER — *Continued*.
    inciting, to resist, 192.
    right to take, through streets naked, 199.
    taking before magistrate, 96, 195.
    may waive right to be taken before magistrate, 102, 197, 280.
    may be released by officer without taking before a magistrate, 97, 102, 197, 280.
    incapacity of, relieves officer from taking before magistrate at once, 96.
    may be killed if necessary to prevent escape, 187.
    may shoot officer in self defence, 86.
    unconvicted must not be shackled to convicted prisoner, 194.
    must be particularly described on face of warrant, 93.
    finding guilty of lesser offence than that charged, 17.
    want of authority for arrest will not protect from prosecution, 14, 15.

PRIVATE PERSON (*See* ARREST),
    arrest by, in felony, 112, 155.
    arrest by, in misdemeanor, 116.
    arrest by, for felony must not be from hearsay information, 112.
    generally obliged to go to officer's assistance, 291, 292.
    may arrest only when felony has actually been committed, 112.
    warrant may be directed to, if necessary, 60.
    may be entitled to assistance, 113.
    may arrest without warrant, 112, 116.
    may use force, 128.
    may kill felon if necessary to prevent escape, 145.
    may break doors on fresh pursuit, 145, 155.

PROBABLE CAUSE,
    necessary to issue of warrant, 56.

PROCESS (*See* WARRANT),
    what is, 12.
    essentials of, to protect officer, 29, 30.
    magistrate must follow law in issuing, 11.

194 INDEX

[References are to sections.]

PROCESS — *Continued.*
    is void if magistrate has no jurisdiction, 16.
    serving improperly may be false imprisonment, 279.
    authority to serve may not be delegated by a deputy, 62.

PROSTITUTE,
    soliciting by, is breach of the peace, 124.
    officer has no right to arrest on common reputation of, 124.
    charging one with being, is not a breach of the peace, 125.

PROTECTION,
    , writ of, is only prima facie proof of exemption, 263.

R.

READING WARRANT,
    to prisoner may be necessary, 78.

RENDITION (*See* EXTRADITION),
    what is inter-state, 222.
    can only be for crime, 225.
    difference between rendition and extradition, 204.
    fugitive may be arrested before proceedings are begun in, 223.
    fugitive may be tried for any crime, 220.
    preliminaries to starting proceedings in, 224.
    jurisdiction in, procured by stratagem, 221.
    will not lie for bastardy, 225.
    will not be ordered for trivial offences, 222.
    one under bail in, may not be re-arrested, 220.
    duty to surrender in, is obligatory, 226.
    who is fugitive from justice in, 227.

RESCUE,
    return of, 36.

RESISTING (*See* INTERFERENCE),
    illegal arrest, 86.
    right to kill one resisting legal arrest, 86, 92, 185, 190.
    person resisting is not entitled to see warrant, 78.

INDEX 195

[References are to sections.]

RESTRAINT,
is necessary to secure personal liberty, 8.
of person is necessary to arrest, 73.

RETURN,
of warrant is necessary to its validity, 34.
without return officer is not protected, 34.
may be amended by officer with permission of court, 36.
effect of return as against officer, 36.
effect of return as against parties, 36.
of rescue, 36.

ROUGHNESS (*See* FORCE),
when not necessary is unjustifiable, 186.

S.

SEAL,
is not necessary to warrant at common law, 50.
is necessary on warrant only when statute requires it, 45, 50, 93.

SEARCHING PRISONER,
right to search prisoner, 200.
may be at time of arrest, 202.
removing clothing in, 200.
no right to remove ordinary money and valuables in, 200.

SEARCH WARRANT,
definition of, 21.
how issued, 22.
may be issued to search a person, 22.
permission will justify searching without a warrant, 24.
illegal seizure under, does not destroy admissibility of evidence obtained thereby, 24a.
issues to recover what, 22, 25.
provisions of United States Constitution, relating to, 23.
United States Constitution, does not apply to searches made by State authorities, 23.

STATUTE,
abrogates common law, 13.
authorizing civil arrest, 104.

[References are to sections.]

STATUTE — *Continued.*
    giving jurisdiction implies power to arrest, 59.
    if unconstitutional, cannot give jurisdiction, 16, 289.
    generally regulates search warrants, 25.
    may authorize general arrest without warrant, 38.
    in absence of, warrant may issue on Sunday, 47.
    warrant is valid only in issuing county in absence of, 49.
    usually provides who may issue warrants, 55.
    authority given by, must be followed strictly, 289.
    unless required by, complaint need not be in writing, 54.
    must not be construed so as to multiply felonies, 115.
    may require seal on warrant, 50, 93.
    exemptions existing by statute, 269, 270.

STOLEN GOODS,
    possession of, as evidence, 242a.

SUBSCRIBED,
    means written beneath, 58.

SUNDAY,
    warrants may issue on, 47.
    no civil arrest can be made on, 47, 76.
    arrest for conspiracy may be on, 261.
    arrest for felony may be on, 47, 76.

SUSPICION,
    arrest on reasonable, 73, 129.

T.

TERRITORY,
    jurisdiction over ceded, 19.

THREATS,
    evidence of, 242.
    may justify arrest, 121.

TRESPASS (*See* FALSE IMPRISONMENT, ARREST),
    what is, 283.
    trespass "*vi et armis,*" 284.
    will lie for an unintentional act, 285.
    will not lie for an accidental act, 285.
    criminal action will lie only when criminal intent exists, 286.

INDEX

[References are to sections.]

TRESPASS — *Continued.*
trespass "*ab initio*," 294, 295.
ab initio does not apply to criminal cases, 295.
in entry by permission of party, 295.

TRESPASSER,
who is a, 283,

U.

UNIFORM,
is notice that wearer is an officer, 81.

V.

VAGRANCY,
arrest for, 142.

VESSELS,
jurisdiction over foreign, 18.

W.

WAIVER,
prisoner may waive right to be taken before magistrate, 102, 197, 280.

WARRANT (*See* PROCESS, ARREST, OFFICER),
search warrant, 21, 55.
bench warrant, 26.
of arrest, 27.
life of, 35.
requisites of a, valid, 45, 93.
requisites of, in extradition, 209.
who may apply for, 53.
who may issue, 55.
must not be issued without complaint, 52, 56.
who may issue in extradition, 207, 208.
will not protect officer unless issued to him, 44.
must not be issued in blank, 37.
in issuing, law must be followed strictly, 11.
arrest with, 90 *et seq.*
arrest with is preferable, 20.

[References are to sections.]

WARRANT—*Continued.*
    officer need not imperil, 79.
    need not be shown unless demanded, 82.
    officer need not part with possession of, 79.
    when officer is not obliged to show, 78, 79.
    when person arrested is entitled to see, 78.
    must be in possession of officer at time of arrest, 46.
    when void, 37, 38, 56, 93.
    what it must show, 45.
    must *command* arrest, 45.
    to whom it should be directed, 60, 61.
    may be directed to a private person, 60.
    may be directed to officer by name or description of office, 61.
    mere reading will not constitute arrest, 67.
    must name or describe party to be arrested, 90, 279.
    actual notice of authority obviates necessity of reading, 83.
    will justify arrest of one named only, 93.
    if not valid, officer is a trespasser, 92.
    when protection to, 29, 91.
    arrest on lawful for unlawful purpose, 279.
    need not state when prisoner is to be brought before magistrate, 96.
    will not protect officer unless magistrate has general jurisdiction, 30.
    arrest may be on old warrant not returned, 35.
    escaped prisoner may be taken on same or without any warrant, 89.
    endorsing warrant to arrest in another county, 49.
    can be no escape on void, 89.
    may be altered only by issuing magistrate, 48.
    may be issued on Sunday, except, 47.
    remains in force until returned, 35.
    to arrest fugitive in another State, 214.
    general warrants are void, 38, 41.
    arrest without, 112 *et seq.*